The
ABCs
of the
UCC

Article 1:
General Provisions

Second Edition

Scott J. Burnham

Business Law Section
AMERICAN BAR ASSOCIATION

Cover design by Bobbie Sanchez/ABA Publishing.

Page layout by Quadrum Solutions.

The materials contained herein represent the opinions of the authors and editors and should not be construed to be the views or opinions of the law firms or companies with whom such persons are in partnership with, associated with, or employed by, nor of the American Bar Association or the Business Law Section unless adopted pursuant to the bylaws of the Association.

Nothing contained in this book is to be considered as the rendering of legal advice for specific cases, and readers are responsible for obtaining such advice from their own legal counsel. This book and any forms and agreements herein are intended for educational and informational purposes only.

Printed in the United States of America.

17 16 15 14 13   5 4 3 2 1

Library of Congress Cataloging-in-Publication Data

Burnham, Scott J.

ABCs of the UCC. Article 1 / Scott J. Burnham. — 2013 edition.

pages cm

Includes bibliographical references and index.

ISBN 978-1-61438-948-4 (alk. paper)

1. Commercial law—United States—States. I. Title. II. Title: Article 1.

KF889.85.B87 2013

346.7307—dc23

2013005580

Discounts are available for books ordered in bulk. Special consideration is given to state bars, CLE programs, and other bar related organizations. Inquire at Book Publishing, ABA Publishing, American Bar Association, 321 N. Clark Street, Chicago, Illinois 60654-7598.

www.ShopABA.org

CONTENTS

Chapter 4

Chapter 5

Chapter 6

Chapter 7

Chapter 8

Chapter 9

Chapter 10

Chapter 11

Chapter 12

Chapter 13

Chapter 14

Chapter 15

Chapter 16

Chapter 17

Chapter 18

Chapter 19

Chapter 20

ACKNOWLEDGEMENTS

I am indebted to Fred H. Miller, past Executive Director of the Uniform Law Commission, who authored the first edition of this work. I am also grateful for the research assistance of Sara Hurn, a student at Gonzaga University School of Law. I am responsible for any errors or omissions in the work.

Scott J. Burnham
Curley Professor of Commercial Law
Gonzaga University School of Law
Editor

FOREWORD

Since it was first proposed over seventy years ago, the Uniform Commercial Code has become both an indispensable part of the study of law and an essential part of legal practice. Adopted by all fifty states, the Code has been hailed as one of the great products of American law. Its impact is by no means limited to the United States. The Code has become one an important United States export: other nations have modeled their laws after our Uniform Commercial Code, and portions of the Code and its principles have been carried over into international instruments such as the United Nations Convention on the International Sale of Goods, the United Nations Convention on the Assignment of Receivables in International Trade, and the UNIDROIT Convention on International Interests in Mobile Equipment.

Despite the importance and impact of the Code, many practitioners and students find it difficult to master. Its provisions, followed by official comments, cross-references, and notes, often seem impenetrable. The problem stems from several sources.

First, as Grant Gilmore once observed, the Code sometimes appears to have been written in its own shorthand. The keys to deciphering that shorthand are frequently found in the definitions to the Code and are often found in an understanding of non-Code law.

Second, no single provision of the Code can truly be understood without an understanding of the other provisions of the Code and its overarching purposes, policies, and concepts. The interconnectedness of the Code's provisions and the importance of its often unarticulated policies require extended study for mastery.

Third, the Code, even on its own terms, does not purport to contain all the law there is on a particular subject; the Code may be uniform, but it is not comprehensive. The Code invites us to consult non-Code law to "fill in the gaps" in its coverage.

Last, the Uniform Commercial Code itself is not "law." Rather, the Code is adopted on a state-by-state basis; individual states may make non-uniform amendments during the adoption process, or state courts may interpret its provisions in a non-uniform manner, making it all the more difficult for the new practitioner or student to master.

This series of books, *The ABCs of the UCC,* a project of the Uniform Commercial Code Committee of the American Bar Association's Section of Business Law, has been making the Code accessible to practitioner and student alike for almost fifteen years. Free of the footnotes and the extensive convoluted discussions that often accompany legal literature, each book is written to present the basic concepts and operation of the Code articles in a simple, straightforward manner. No attempt is made to treat the Code in an in-depth manner, nor to cite to all possibly relevant authorities and cases. Rather, the goal is to provide the reader with the framework and basic knowledge of the Code necessary to orient the reader for future work or research. Thus, this series of books does not supplant, but rather complements, more intensive treatments of the subjects.

Each book in the series is devoted to one of the articles of the Code, yet they are intended to form a coherent whole, which, taken together, provides an overview of the Code in operation. Each book is written by a distinguished person in the field of commercial law who is considered an expert in the field by colleagues. The focus is on the uniform text of the Code: the text as adopted by the sponsors of the Code, the American Law Institute and the Uniform Law Commission. While the focus is on the uniform version, each book, where appropriate, points out important non-uniform amendments and divergent judicial treatment of the Code provisions.

In 1965, Grant Gilmore warned that the enactment of the Code and of Article 9 did not mark the end of the process of change and development in the field of commercial law. His comments were more perceptive than he could have realized. Since his prescient words were penned, the Code has undergone extensive revision and change: new articles were added, others replaced or amended, and one has even been repealed. The well-advised practitioner and student realize that the process of learning should be an ongoing one; the knowledge gained from their reading of this current series of ready reference books should nonetheless provide a firm foundation for supplementation in the future.

The Uniform Commercial Code Committee of the ABA's Section of Business Law welcomes the opportunity to provide these tools to the legal profession. We hope that you find this series of books useful for your needs.

Amelia H. Boss
Drexel University Earle Mack School of Law
Series Editor

PREFACE

This primer provides an introduction to the Uniform Commercial Code (UCC or Code) and discusses the provisions of its first article, Article 1 General Provisions. While each subsequent article of the Code focuses on a different type of commercial transaction, Article 1 contains general principles and definitions that apply throughout the Code.

Article 1 is central to the Code, like the hub of a wheel, and the substantive articles that follow it are tied together, through the first article, like spokes. Therefore, one cannot fully understand the substantive articles of the Code without considering the applicable provisions in its central article, Article 1.

This primer provides a convenient starting point for a person embarking on a study of the primary issues and concepts in the Code. One may also benefit from the primer as an overview of the substance of Article 1. A more thorough scrutiny of the Code, related cases, and commentary is essential for those who need to advise a client or litigate issues involving the substantive articles of the Code.

There is no inherent order to the sections of Article 1. However, Article 1 is divided into three parts that emphasize different matters. Part 1 (General Provisions) includes sections that deal with the scope and proper interpretation of the Code (§§ 1-102 through 1-107) and its relationship to federal law (§ 1-108). Part 2 (General Definitions and Principles of Interpretation) consists of definitions (§§ 1-201 through 1-204), timing (§ 1-205), and procedure (§ 1-206). Part 3 (Territorial Applicability and General Rules) includes substantive provisions that either confer on parties the power to do things or limit agreements or action (§§ 1-301 through 1-304, 1-306, 1-308, and 1-309). This third part also contains sections one might classify as administrative (§§ 1-305, 1-307, and 1-310). By reviewing together sections within a suggested group, one can gain a sense of context, and context is an important consideration in understanding the Code.

This primer is based on the 2011 Official Text of Article 1, which includes changes made since its initial promulgation in 2001 to conform to amendments to other articles. Because it has become the norm, this primer will refer to that text as "Article 1" except where it is helpful to avoid confusion, in which case the Pre-2001 text will be referred to as "Former Article 1," and the Post-2001 text will be referred to as "Revised Article 1." Of course, the user will need to determine whether a particular jurisdiction has enacted Revised Article 1. A table of enacting jurisdictions can be found by clicking on UCC Article 1, General Provisions (2001) under "Acts" at the Uniform Law Commission website, http://www.uniformlaws.org. Furthermore, the user will need to determine the extent to which a jurisdiction has enacted nonuniform versions of the provisions. Some of the more significant state variations are identified in this primer. For more information on nonuniform enactments, see the Local Code Variations in the Uniform Commercial Code Reporting Service.

The drafters of Revised Article 1 reorganized the sections and in some instances changed the section numbers of Former Article 1. The accompanying table may assist the user in locating the former sections.

Article 1 Section Reorganization

Former Article 1	Revised Article 1
§ 1-101	§ 1-101
None	§ 1-102
§ 1-102(1) & (2)	§ 1-103(a)
§ 1-102(3) & (4)	§ 1-302(a) and (c)
§ 1-102(5)	§ 1-106
§ 1-103	§ 1-103(b)
§ 1-104	§ 1-104
§ 1-105	§ 1-301
§ 1-106	§ 1-305

Former Article 1	Revised Article 1
§ 1-107	§ 1-306
§ 1-108	§ 1-105
§ 1-109	§ 1-107
None	§ 1-108
§ 1-201(25),(26),(27)	§ 1-202
§ 1-201(31)	§ 1-206
§ 1-201(37)	§§ 1-201(b)(35), 1-203
§ 1-201(44)	§ 1-204
§ 1-201(remainder)	§ 1-201
§ 1-202	§ 1-307
§ 1-203	§ 1-304
§ 1-204(1)	§ 1-302(b)
§ 1-204(2) & (3)	§ 1-205
§ 1-205	§ 1-303
§ 1-206	Deleted
§ 1-207	§ 1-308
§ 1-208	§ 1-309
§ 1-209	§ 1-310

Note that §§ 1-102 (Scope of Article) and 1-108 (Relation to Electronic Signatures in Global and National Commerce Act) of Revised Article 1 have no prior counterpart. Former § 1-206 was deleted; the substance of Revised § 1-206 was formerly found in § 1-201(31).

CHAPTER

1

THE UNIFORM COMMERCIAL CODE: HISTORY, OVERVIEW, AND CITATION

A. Introduction

Commercial transactions in all states, the District of Columbia, Puerto Rico, and the U.S. Virgin Islands are governed by the Uniform Commercial Code (UCC or Code).

The term "commercial transaction" is not defined in the Code, but it can be thought of as covering a wide range of business activities. It includes sales and leases of goods, transfers of negotiable instruments such as promissory notes and checks, payments made by wire transfer or letter of credit, transactions covering the shipment or storage of goods, transfers of investment property like stocks and bonds, and transfers for the more limited purpose of securing an obligation. That subset of commercial transactions called consumer transactions—transactions entered into for personal, family, or household purposes—is generally governed by the same Code rules unless otherwise indicated.

Courts, however, are often asked to determine whether it is consistent with the purpose of a Code rule to apply it in the same way to a consumer. See, e.g., Official Comment 4 to § 2-607 (providing that a buyer must notify a seller of a breach within a reasonable time), which states in part:

> "A reasonable time" for notification from a retail consumer is to be judged by different standards so that in his case it will be extended, for the rule of requiring notification is designed to defeat commercial bad faith, not to deprive a good faith consumer of his remedy.

Although Congress has the power to regulate interstate commerce, it has largely left the task of developing the law of commercial transactions to the states. Therefore, the Code is state law, developed by two organizations engaged in law reform, the Uniform Law Commission (ULC) (formerly known as the National Conference of Commissioners on Uniform State Laws (NCCUSL)) and the American Law Institute (ALI). Most of the Code has been enacted by the legislatures of the 50 states, the District of Columbia, Puerto Rico, and the U.S. Virgin Islands. See the Uniform Law Commission website, http://www.uniformlaws.org for a list of enactments.

The objectives of the Code are to promote uniformity in the commercial laws of the various states, to simplify, clarify, and modernize the law of commercial transactions, and to permit the continued expansion of commercial practices by custom, usage, and agreement of the parties. § 1-103(a). Having the law in the form of the Code reduces transaction risks and costs in two ways: the law is easier to find in the Code than in scattered decisions or statutes, and the quality of the draftsmanship and the research behind it reduce ambiguity and omitted cases that may result in litigation.

B. History

As the discussion in this book indicates, the Code is a living body of law. It is frequently revised by its sponsoring groups and it is stretched to apply to evolving transactions. The Code first began to be enacted in the 1960s. Subsequent amendments to the original Code were made to address concerns raised by the New York Law Revision Commission. Later amendments addressed nonuniform amendments to Article 9, particularly involving fixtures, and worries over conflicts between accounts lenders and inventory lenders. Still later amendments were made to accommodate uncertificated securities.

By the early 1980s, changes in technology and business practices were placing heavy pressure on the Code's expansion joints (the general ability to set a rule by agreement, practice, and course of dealing). The leasing of goods had grown in importance to the point that application by analogy of the rules for sales no longer sufficed, and variable rate promissory notes were being interpreted out of Article 3. Millions of dollars were being transferred electronically without statutory rules, and the automated processing of checks was accomplished under agreement more than under the statute. These developments, as well as growing litigation as ambiguities in the statute were discovered or exploited, led to ongoing revision of the Code.

Addressing these matters at times has proven to be extraordinarily difficult. In the 1990s, a situation much like that which existed for leases of goods developed concerning transactions in computer information. After a period, the effort to draft a statute to govern such transactions took the form of a proposed new Article 2B to the Code. That effort finally floundered over disagreement concerning a number of provisions of the proposed article, which perhaps could not be reconciled due to fundamental differences in underlying philosophy concerning the proper role for commercial law.

Ultimately, the ULC brought proposed Article 2B forward, not as part of the Code, but as the freestanding Uniform Computer Information Transactions Act (UCITA). UCITA was enacted in only two states, however, before it was withdrawn. The differences that led to that development were revisited in debate over the scope section of Article 2. Revised versions of Article 2 and Article 2A were withdrawn, as were the less ambitious Amended Article 2 and Amended Article 2A. What this sort of difficulty portends for the future is not fully comprehensible at this time. It is clear, however, that attention to the Code will continue to occupy the sponsoring organizations.

In the meantime, practitioners may well find themselves arguing that Code concepts should be applied by analogy to non-Code transactions such as software transactions. The ALI's *Principles of Software Contracts*, for example, demonstrates the applicability of many Code concepts to software transactions.

For more on the role of the ULC, see the Appendix.

C. Overview

Turning to an overview of the Code itself, the statute now comprises thirteen articles, two of which deal with transition and are omitted from this overview:

- **Article 1** contains general definitions and principles applicable to all articles.
- **Article 2** deals basically with the sale of goods. Although efforts to revise Article 2 have been withdrawn, some provisions have been revised through conforming amendments when other articles have been revised.
- **Article 2A** governs leases of goods. Prior to the promulgation of Article 2A in 1987, the provisions of Article 2 were frequently applied by analogy to leases. Most states have adopted Article 2A, and the law of leasing has finally received substantially uniform codification. As with Article 2, although efforts to revise Article 2A have been withdrawn, some provisions have been revised through conforming amendments when other articles have been revised.
- **Article 3** primarily deals with checks and promissory notes, the two main types of negotiable instruments, formerly

called commercial paper. The article also deals with drafts and many written certificates of deposit. It governs the rights and liabilities of parties who make, use, and receive such paper. Some limited amendments to this article were promulgated in 2002.

* **Article 4** governs bank deposits and collections with respect to checks, drafts, and other items in the payment process. Federal Regulation CC on funds availability has had a substantial impact in this area, and check collections are subject to both state law (Article 4) and federal regulation. Some limited amendments to this article were promulgated in 2002.

* **Article 4A** deals with a more modern means of payment— electronic funds transfers in a commercial setting.

* **Article 5** deals with letters of credit, a device frequently used as a payment mechanism. A letter of credit is like a guarantee but with a major difference: the letter of credit issuer's obligation is independent of the transaction for which the letter of credit was issued.

* **Article 6** is an offshoot of Article 2 for a specialized type of sale, a bulk sale. Pursuant to the recommendation of the ULC and the ALI, it has been repealed in a majority of states and continues, in revised form, in only a few states.

* **Article 7** deals with documents of title that are not governed by federal law. It covers the rights of parties in shipments using bills of lading or in storage using warehouse receipts. These documents of title are often used as collateral under Article 9. A revised version of Article 7 was promulgated in 2003.

* **Article 8** deals with investment securities (stocks and bonds), whether held in paper form, in uncertificated form, or indirectly in a brokerage account or other book entry format.

* **Article 9** deals with security interests in personal property that are granted by agreement. It also governs certain liens

created by law rather than by agreement. It was revised in 1998 and additional amendments were promulgated in 2010.

D. Research Techniques

There are many complexities involved in citing UCC authority to a court. First, the Code changes vertically over time as a jurisdiction enacts the revisions outlined in the Overview section. Second, the Code changes horizontally as jurisdictions enact nonuniform versions of the uniform text. Let's look at each of these considerations in turn.

When citing authority from your own jurisdiction, make sure you are finding the relevant Code section when finding and citing older cases, for the section number might have changed during the revision process. For example, as indicated in the chart in the Preface, former § 1-107 is now § 1-306; pre-revision § 9-312(3) and (4) is now § 9-324. More importantly, once you have found the relevant section, make sure the substance has not changed. For example, the definition of "good faith" in former § 1-201(19) differs substantively from the definition in revised § 1-201(b)(20).

Authority from other jurisdictions can be more persuasive in a Code case than in non-Code cases because of the Code's central purpose of uniformity set out in § 1-103(a)(3). This purpose might persuade a court to follow the majority interpretation of a Code provision. For example, in *Northrop Corp. v. Litronic Industries*, 29 F.3d 1173, 24 U.C.C. Rep. Serv. 2d 407 (7th Cir. 1994), a diversity case in which the court had to decide what the appropriate Illinois rule should be, Judge Posner agreed to an interpretation that he did not favor because most states went along with that interpretation and Illinois appropriately followed the majority when deciding how to interpret a Code provision.

Because state legislatures have the power to make changes to the language of the uniform text of the Code, it is especially important to check whether the language of the Code section you are citing is the same in the cited jurisdiction as it is in your jurisdiction. For example, assume you are looking for authority to argue that the language "[T]he additional terms are to be construed as proposals for addition to the contract" in § 2-207(2) should be interpreted to include "different terms." You come across a Montana case that holds that § 2-207(2) applies to both additional terms and different terms. You should not cite that case as authority, because the Montana legislature enacted a nonuniform version of § 2-207(2) that expressly provides that the section is applicable to "additional or different terms." Thus, because the text of the Code differs, the Montana case does not support your interpretation argument.

When citing federal cases, you should keep in mind that because the Code is state law, a federal court generally has jurisdiction over a Code matter because of diversity. Thus, a federal court opinion may have limited precedential value. For example, assume your jurisdiction is Arizona, which is in the Ninth Circuit, and you find a Ninth Circuit case on point. That case is not mandatory authority for a state court in Arizona—in fact, it may not even be highly persuasive. Always check the federal case to see which state's law is being applied. If the Ninth Circuit decision is applying Washington law, then the decision is only persuasive in Arizona. In fact, even if the Ninth Circuit decision is applying Arizona law, it is not necessarily highly persuasive.

In fact, the federal court puts itself in the shoes of the highest state court and tries to determine how that court is likely to rule. But because the issue is a matter of state law, if a state court encounters the same issue decided by the federal court, the state court is perfectly free to rule in a contrary manner.

When citing the Code as authority, check to see if the issue was addressed in a Code revision, even if the revision was never enacted. For example, Amended Article 2 has been withdrawn, but many sections of that proposed draft resolved ambiguities and filled in gaps in enacted Article 2. See, e.g., Amended § 2-725, which clarified many unresolved issues regarding the statute of limitations in the enacted section. Although an attorney could not cite the unenacted version of a statute as mandatory authority, the fact that it expressed the view of the experts who drafted the Code can be persuasive on the issue of how to interpret and fill in gaps in the enacted provision. These drafts can be found at the ULC website, http://uniformlaws.org.

A UCC Research Guide can be found in the Information tab under Links and Resources at the website of the Commercial Law Center at http://www.law.gonzaga.edu/centers-programs/commercial-law/links-resources/

CHAPTER

2

Using the Code and Comments

A. The Definitions

The most challenging aspect of using the Code, until you become used to it, is always remembering to check whether a word or phrase used in a Code section is defined in the Code.

Section 1-201 contains definitions of a great number of terms used throughout the Code. Similar, but more detailed, definitions are found in §§ 1-202 through 1-204. Furthermore, each Code article is divided into parts, and Part 1 of each article may contain definitions and general principles peculiar to that article. If a term is not defined in Article 1, Part 1 of the substantive article may contain a definition of the term. See, e.g., §§ 2-103(1) and 9-102(a).

On occasion, the definition in one substantive article may differ from the definition in another. For example, "goods" is defined for purposes of Article 2 in § 2-105(1) and for purposes of Article 9 in § 9-102(a)(44). If the term is defined in both Article 1 and a substantive article, then the definition in the substantive article trumps the Article 1 definition. For example, the definition of "good faith" in § 5-102(a)(7) differs from the definition in § 1-201(b)(20) and would govern in an Article 5 transaction.

Part 1 of each of the substantive articles of the Code has an index of relevant defined terms found in other parts of the Code. See, e.g., §§ 2-103(3) and 9-102(b). Each substantive section of the Code is followed by definitional cross-references that direct the reader to definitions of terms used in that section. These cross-references are not always complete, however, and the absence of a term from the definitional cross-references does not mean that it is not a defined term.

The importance of Code definitions cannot be overemphasized because the definitions may affect the meaning of substantive provisions. To illustrate, § 1-201(b)(9) defines a "buyer in ordinary course of business," which is a key concept in many sections, such as §§ 2-403(2) and 9-320(a). It is not, however, the same concept as a "bona fide purchaser"; rather, it is a bona fide purchaser from inventory.

Moreover, to understand a definition, other defined words used in the definition must be understood. For example, the first sentence of § 1-201(b)(9), defining "buyer in ordinary course of business" (ignoring the fact that for purposes of Article 2, the term "buyer" itself is defined in § 2-103(1)(a)), contains seven other terms that are defined either in Article 1 or a subsequent article. If these additional defined terms were set in boldface, the sentence would look like this:

> "Buyer in ordinary course of business" means a **person** that **buys goods** in **good faith,** without **knowledge** that the **sale** violates the **rights** of another **person** in the **goods,** and in the ordinary course from a **person,** other than a pawnbroker, in the business of selling **goods** of that kind.

To understand the definition of "buyer in ordinary course of business," therefore, these other defined words must be understood. Cross-referencing these terms with the Code sections in which they are defined would make this first sentence of § 1-201(b)(9) read like this:

"Buyer in ordinary course of business" means a **person** (under § 1-201(b)(27), this includes an individual or an organization; "organization" under § 1-201(b)(25) includes "a corporation, government or governmental subdivision or agency, business trust, estate, trust, partnership or association, two or more persons having a joint or common interest, or any other legal or commercial entity") that **buys** (see § 1-201(b)(9) itself and, as involving terms in the definition of "buying," *see also* "document of title" at § 1-201(b)(16), "contract for sale" at § 2-106(1), and "bulk sale" at § 6-102(1)) **goods** (defined somewhat differently in §§ 2-105(1), 2A-103(l)(h), and § 9-105(l)(h)) in **good faith** (which means under § 1-201(b)(20) honesty in fact, and except in Article 5, the observance of reasonable commercial standards of fair dealing) without **knowledge** (which means under § 1-202 actual knowledge) that the **sale** (defined in § 2-106(1)) violates the **rights** (see § 1-201(b) (34) and (32)) of another **person** (see above) in the **goods** (see above), and in the ordinary course (not explicitly defined, but compare § 2-402(3)(b) with § 6-102(l)(m)) from a **person** (see above), other than a pawnbroker, in the business of selling **goods** (see above) of that kind.

Again, the importance of consulting the definitional sections of the Code cannot be overstated. The definitions are precise and at times contain more of the substance of a rule or principle than the section in which the rule or principle is apparently stated. Keep in mind that defined terms were bold-faced here for purposes of illustration. In the text of the Code, however, it is not always obvious when one is dealing with a defined term. Therefore, it is doubly important to consult the definitional cross-references following each substantive section.

B. The Official Comments

Most Code sections are followed by "Official Comments." The comments were originally designed to allow nonlawyers to understand the statute, but they are also useful to lawyers in putting the section in context, elaborating on the principles involved in the section, and guiding interpretation to preserve uniformity.

The comments may demonstrate how a number of complicated sections fit together. For example, § 2A-301 Official Comment 3 provides a hypothetical illustration of how the provisions of Part 3 of Article 2A interrelate. For clarity's sake, the comments may also explore the application of the statute to concrete fact situations. For example, § 2-314 Official Comments 1 and 3 indicate that the implied warranty of merchantability applies both to sales for resale as well as sales for use, and to sales of second-hand goods as well as sales of new goods. The statutory language of § 2-314 certainly supports these comments, but is not specific. Thus, these comments answer two possible questions that arise from the provision. Note that the comments do not address the applicable standard for used goods; for matters of that nature, one must turn to the cases. See, e.g., *Dickerson v. Mt. View Equip. Co.,* 710 P.2d 621, 42 U.C.C. Rep. Serv. 114 (Idaho Ct. App. 1985).

The comments also may be helpful by directing the reader to other Code provisions that illuminate other aspects of the matter. For example, Official Comment 4 to § 9-101 summarizes the changes made by the 1998 revision to Article 9, and illustrates where the rules with respect to each type of collateral may be found.

The comments to the Code are prepared by the reporter for the article, with the guidance of the drafting committee chair, around the time the article is promulgated by the Code sponsors. They should, therefore, be considered persuasive elaboration on the provision. However, because all the comments may not be before the ULC and the ALI when those bodies consider the final draft of an article, they cannot be said to positively reflect the understanding of the Code sponsors. Also, in most cases, they are not before a state legislature when it considers the article for enactment.

Because Official Comments are not enacted by the individual state legislatures, they are therefore *not the law*, except in the rare case that a state legislature has adopted the comments. In Kentucky, for example, KRS § 355.1-103(3) provides:

> Official comments to the Uniform Commercial Code, as published from time to time by the National Conference of Commissioners on Uniform State Laws, represent the express legislative intent of the General Assembly and shall be used as a guide for interpretation of this chapter, except that if the text and the official comments conflict, the text shall control.

Section 1-101(3)(f) of the 1953 text of the Code provided in essence that the comments could be consulted in the construction and application of the Code but, if text and comment conflicted, the text would control. The section was later deleted, however, leaving the question of what role the comments play open to interpretation. A notorious example of text and comment conflicting is Official Comment 3 to § 2-207. The comment states:

> Whether or not additional or different terms will become part of the agreement depends upon the provisions of subsection (2).

Subsection (2), however, refers to "additional terms" but is silent on different terms.

While the comments are intended to help with a basic understanding of the statute, courts have added to the interpretations of their role. See, in support of comments adding value, *In re Peregrine Entertainment, Ltd.,* 116 B.R. 194, 11 U.C.C. Rep. Serv. 2d 1025 (C.D. Cal. 1990) (comments are persuasive); *Simmons v. Clemco Industries,* 368 So. 2d 509, 25 U.C.C. Rep. Serv. 1088 (Ala. 1979) (comments are a valuable aid in construction but not enacted by legislature and cannot revise clear language of statute); *Morrow v. New Moon Homes, Inc.,* 548 P.2d 279, 19 U.C.C. Rep. Serv. 1

(Alaska 1976) (comments are not necessarily controlling but are of persuasive assistance in construction and application); *Thompson v. United States,* 408 F.2d 1075, 6 U.C.C. Rep. Serv. 20 (8th Cir. 1969) (applying Arkansas law) (same as preceding case); and *Title Ins. Co. of Minnesota v. Comerica Bank-California,* 27 Cal. App. 4th 800, 32 Cal. Rptr. 2d 735, 24 U.C.C. Rep. Serv. 2d 584 (1994) (comments used to reach correct understanding of statute). On the other hand, when a court does not agree with a comment, it need not follow it. See, e.g., *In re M & S Grading, Inc.*, 457 F.3d 898, 60 U.C.C. Rep. Serv. 2d 295 (8th Cir. 2006) (applying Nebraska law) ("courts are bound by statutes, not statutory commentary") and *Hartford Fire Insurance Co. v. Maryland National Bank, N.A.,* 341 Md. 408, 671 A.2d 22, 28 U.C.C. Rep. Serv. 2d 767 (Ct. App. Md. 1996) (reaching a result directly contradictory to a Code comment without even mentioning the comment).

As the authorities make clear, the comments cannot change the meaning of the statute. Thus, one should always be certain the statute supports the comment. To illustrate this point, § 1-306 provides that "[a] claim or right arising out of an alleged breach may be discharged in whole or in part without consideration by agreement of the aggrieved party in an authenticated record." The literal wording of § 1-306 seems to state that a merchant or a consumer with equal facility may sign a release for a claim for breach of warranty. Official Comment 1, however, states that the section applies to "an alleged breach of a *commercial* contract," perhaps suggesting that the section does not apply to *consumer* contracts. Alternatively, one could simply interpret the word "commercial" as referring to the types of transactions covered by the Code, which include transactions in which consumers are parties. Clearly one should not read § 1-306 to disallow waivers by consumers. One might interpret the comment, however, as signaling that consumer waivers are likely to be more closely scrutinized, or even regulated by other law. See, e.g., 1974 Uniform Consumer Credit Code § 1.107(4).

Perhaps the most famous comment that went beyond the scope of the statute was former § 2-507 Official Comment 3, which mentioned a time frame of ten days. One could look in vain in the statute without finding the ten days the comment mentioned. Courts split as to whether to follow it, and the Permanent Editorial Board for the UCC in PEB Commentary No. 1 overruled the ultra vires time frame stated in the former comment. Another example is Official Comment 5 to § 9-204, which states in part:

> Determining the obligations secured by collateral is solely a matter of construing the parties' agreement under applicable law. This Article rejects the holdings of cases decided under former Article 9 that applied other tests, such as whether a future advance or other subsequently incurred obligation was of the same or a similar type or class as earlier advances and obligations secured by the collateral.

In fact, the text of the Code does not reject those holdings.

C. PEB Commentaries

Permanent Editorial Board (PEB) Commentaries, like Official Comments, are a useful interpretive device, but they are of a more recent vintage. Over the years, various ambiguities in a statute may surface, and the PEB issues commentaries in order to resolve those ambiguities. Official Comments address statutes at the time they are promulgated, while PEB Commentaries address the statutes after they are promulgated. The goals of the PEB Commentaries were set forth in a 1987 resolution:

> b. The underlying purposes and policies of the *PEB Commentary* are those specified in [UCC § 1-103(a)]. A *PEB Commentary* should come within one or more of the following specific purposes, which should be made apparent at the inception of the Commentary: (1) to resolve an

ambiguity in the UCC by restating more clearly what the PEB considers to be the legal rule; (2) to state a preferred resolution of an issue on which judicial opinion or scholarly writing diverges; (3) to elaborate on the application of the UCC where the statute and/or the Official Comment leaves doubt as to inclusion or exclusion of, or application to, particular circumstances or transactions; (4) consistent with [UCC § 1-103(a)], to apply the principles of the UCC to new or changed circumstances; (5) to clarify or elaborate upon the operation of the UCC as it relates to other statutes (such as the Bankruptcy Code and various federal and state consumer protection statutes) and general principles of law and equity pursuant to UCC § 1-103[(b)]; or (6) to otherwise improve the operation of the UCC.

Any changes in the original comment as a result of a PEB Commentary may be highlighted in the revised comment. See, e.g., § 2-507 Official Comment 3, discussed in Section B above. Cases utilizing PEB Commentary include *In re LMS Holding Co.,* 153 B.R. 581, 20 U.C.C. Rep. Serv. 2d 1112 (Bankr. N.D. Okla. 1993) (creditors did not have to file new financing statement to remain perfected after sale under facts present in case; PEB Commentary No. 3) and *UNI Imports, Inc. v. Aparacor, Inc.,* 978 F.2d 984, 18 U.C.C. Rep. Serv. 2d 993 (7th Cir. 1992) (applying Illinois law) ("nonadvances" made by a lender to protect and preserve the debtor's assets had priority over the judgment creditor's lien; PEB Commentary No. 2). Some commentaries have been superseded by later amendments or revisions to a statute; for example, PEB Commentary No. 2 by §§ 9-323 and 9-204.

CHAPTER

3

OVERVIEW AND SCOPE OF ARTICLE 1
§§ 1-101 AND 1-102

§ 1-101. Short Titles.

(a)   This [Act] may be cited as the Uniform Commercial Code.

(b)   This article may be cited as Uniform Commercial Code—General Provisions.

§ 1-102. Scope of Article.

This article applies to a transaction to the extent that it is governed by another article of [the Uniform Commercial Code].

A. Introduction

The objectives of the Code are to promote uniformity in the commercial law of the various states; to simplify, clarify, and modernize the law of commercial transactions; and to permit the continued expansion of commercial practices by custom, usage, and agreement of the parties. § 1-103(a). Its widespread adoption and implementation has brought about a level of uniformity throughout the United States not previously achieved in other areas of the law traditionally relegated to the individual states.

B. The Objectives of Uniformity

Despite its adoption by all the states, the Code is not federal law. Thus, transactions with the federal government or its agencies, which must be governed by federal law, are not subject to the Code, although the rules of the Code may be chosen as federal common law. See, e.g., *United States v. Kimbell Foods, Inc.,* 440 U.S. 715 (1979). In addition, because recognized Native American tribes have the power to legislate and their nonstatutory law may be applicable, law other than that of the state in which the tribe is located may be applicable to a commercial transaction. See Fred H. Miller and Duchess Bartmess, *Uniform Laws: Possible Useful Tribal Legislation,* 36 TULSA L.J. 305 (2000). Moreover, commercial transactions are increasingly subject to international rules, which under the U.S. Constitution may preempt state law rules such as the Code. For example, when applicable, the United Nations Convention on Contracts for the International Sale of Goods will displace the Code as governing law.

The objective of uniformity has been compromised to some degree by a number of factors. Not all of the Code has been enacted in Louisiana, Puerto Rico, and the U.S. Virgin Islands, and a few other jurisdictions have not enacted all revisions and amendments. Also, the Code generally is subject to separate consumer protection legislation, which is not uniform. Most importantly, states have made nonuniform changes in the Code. Thus, it is important to determine when or where these sorts of deviations exist. There are several guides available that highlight nonuniform provisions adopted by states, including the Uniform Commercial Code volumes of West's *Uniform Laws Annotated*; Bender's Uniform Commercial Code Service, Reporter-Digest Legislative; and the Uniform Commercial Code Reporting Service, State Correlation Tables.

Despite these deviations, substantial core uniformity exists. While the practitioner must be alert for lagging enactments of revisions or amendments, nonuniform changes, and overriding nonuniform consumer law, these deviations do not represent a serious impediment to the use of the Code.

C. Article 1 and the Other Substantive Articles

Article 1 sets forth the general principles of the UCC and establishes the guidelines for its interpretation. It also provides definitions for many of the Code's terms, although additional terms are defined in the substantive articles that follow it.

As noted in Chapter 1, the main body of the Code consists of substantive articles that cover different types of commercial transactions. These substantive articles are linked through Article 1, and proficiency in the Code requires knowledge of how the provisions are interconnected.

The first section of Article 1 sets forth "short titles." Thus, § 1-101 (a) states:

> This [Act] may be cited as the Uniform Commercial Code.

Of course, this short title probably makes too broad a claim. Even though a state enacts that language, because of nonuniform amendments, it is more accurately enacting the *North Carolina* Commercial Code or the *Montana* Commercial Code. Section 1-101(b) states:

> This article may be cited as Uniform Commercial Code—General Provisions.

Similarly, the first section of each substantive article also states the short title of the article. Section 2-101, for example, states:

> This Article shall be known and may be cited as Uniform Commercial Code—Sales.

D. The Relationship Between UCC and Non-Code Law

The Code does not cover *all* law that may be applicable to a particular transaction. In many situations, non-Code principles of law or equity supplement the Code's provisions. Article 2, for example, contains default rules for many aspects of a sales transaction. These default rules are applicable unless the parties agree to a different rule where the statute allows variance, but other law determines whether entering into the sales contract was authorized. This non-Code law may also impose limitations on the Article 2 rules or on the ability to vary them by agreement in some cases, such as one in which a consumer is involved.

A specific provision in Article 1, § 1-103(b), makes that non-Code law relevant. Thus, issues arising from a given fact pattern falling within a substantive article of the Code cannot always be resolved without consideration of § 1-103(b) and the other law that may be applicable through it. One needs to know non-Code law that applies as well as all relevant provisions of the Code itself. The central issue is when the non-Code law applies and when it is displaced. This issue is discussed in Chapter 5.

E. The Scope of Article 1

Article 1 is not a statute of general application. It applies only to a transaction to the extent the transaction is governed by another article of the Code. § 1-102. The Official Comment to that section, which was added by Revised Article 1, states in part:

> This section makes clear what has always been the case—the rules in Article 1 apply to transactions to the extent that those transactions are governed by one of the other articles of the Uniform Commercial Code.

The section was added because some courts had applied provisions of Article 1 as though they were part of the general law of the jurisdiction, applicable to all transactions. For example, many cases applied former § 1-206, which provided a statute of frauds for the sale of personal property, to non-Code transactions. In *Mellencamp v. Riva Music Ltd.*, 698 F. Supp. 1154 (S.D.N.Y. 1988), for example, the court applied the former Article 1 provision to the transfer of copyrights, which is not a Code transaction.

CODE PURPOSES AND POLICIES
§ 1-103(a)

§ 1-103. Construction of [Uniform Commercial Code] to Promote Its Purposes and Policies; Applicability of Supplemental Principles of Law.

(a)   [The Uniform Commercial Code] must be liberally construed and applied to promote its underlying purposes and policies, which are:

   (1)   to simplify, clarify, and modernize the law governing commercial transactions;

   (2)   to permit the continued expansion of commercial practices through custom, usage, and agreement of the parties; and

   (3)   to make uniform the law among the various jurisdictions.

A. Introduction

Just as an informed reader will always consult definitions and comments when interpreting Code sections, that reader also will rely on the purposes and policies of the Code. Section 1-103(a) may seem to be a relatively innocuous subsection but in fact it contains a very important principle: the Code should be liberally construed and applied to effectuate its purposes and policies.

The guiding principle was stated early by the court in *Lincoln Bank & Trust Co. v. Queenan,* 344 S.W.2d 383, 385, 1 U.C.C. Rep. Serv. 609 (Ky. 1961) (citations omitted):

> The Code represents an entirely new approach in several areas of commercial law, and especially as to security transactions. Its adoption in this state signifies a legislative policy to join with other states in achieving uniformity. The realization of this purpose demands that so far as possible the meaning of the law be gathered from the instrument itself, unfettered by anachronisms indigenous to the respective jurisdictions in which it is in force. Accepting that principle, we adopt as a rule of construction that the Code is plenary and exclusive except where the legislature has clearly indicated otherwise.

What does it mean to "liberally construe" the Code? Those words were seized upon by the Seventh Circuit in *AMF, Inc. v. McDonald's Corp.*, 536 F.2d 1167, 19 U.C.C. Rep. Serv. 801 (7th Cir. 1976). McDonald's claimed that because AMF had not timely responded to its demand for assurances, it could regard AMF as having breached the contract by anticipatory repudiation. But there was a hitch—§ 2-609 requires that the demand be made in writing, and McDonald's had made the demand at a formal meeting between the parties, but had not followed up with a writing. The court dismissed the writing requirement in light of the provision that "the Code shall be liberally construed."

On the one hand, it does not seem reasonable to liberally construe "writing" to mean "not writing." But a careful reading indicates that the provision requires that the Code be liberally construed "to promote its underlying purpose and policies." In other words, a reading that carries out the purpose of the section should prevail over a literal reading. Here, the court found that since the policy behind the writing requirement was to memorialize the demand and to caution the recipient as to its significance, those policies were satisfied by the meeting between the parties. It stated:

> However, AMF urges that Section 2-609 of the UCC is inapplicable because McDonald's did not make a written demand of adequate assurance of due performance. In *Pittsburgh-Des Moines Steel Co. v. Brookhaven Manor Water Co.*, 532 F.2d 572, 581 (7th Cir. 1976), we noted that the Code should be liberally construed and therefore rejected such "a formalistic approach" to Section 2-609. McDonald's failure to make a written demand was excusable because AMF's Mr. Dubosque's testimony and his April 2 and 18, 1969, memoranda about the March 18th meeting showed AMF's clear understanding that McDonald's had suspended performance until it should receive adequate assurance of due performance from AMF (Tr. 395; AMF Exhibit 79; McD. Exhibit 232).

Id. at 1170-71 (footnotes omitted).

B. Modernizing the Law and Expanding Commercial Practices

There is a trend in the interpretation of constitutional law and legislation to slavishly follow the language of the document. The Code, however, counsels against such a limitation in stating that it "must be liberally construed and applied to promote its underlying purposes and policies." Subsection (1) states that one of the Code's purposes and policies is "to simplify, clarify, and modernize the law governing commercial transactions." The Code is intentionally loose in the joints so that it does not have to be frequently amended, even as commercial practices change. Thus, courts should apply it to transactions that may not have even existed at the time of its drafting.

Subsection (2) states that one of the Code's purposes and policies is "to permit the continued expansion of commercial practices through custom, usage, and agreement of the parties." The interpretation of contracts involves a search for the intent of the parties, which is informed not only by their language, but by custom, usage, and the nature of the transaction in which they are involved. This subsection emphasizes the policy of freedom of contract. As further discussed in Chapter 15, the Code consists largely of default rules that the parties are free to change. Furthermore, as further discussed in Chapter 16, custom and usage are part of the parties' agreement as defined by the Code.

C. Uniformity

Subsection (3) states that one of the Code's purposes and policies is "to make uniform the law among the various jurisdictions." To illustrate the operation of this subsection, consider *Sesow v. Swearingen,* 552 P.2d 705, 19 U.C.C. Rep. Serv. 1160 (Okla. 1976). In that case, prior to December 5, 1972, goods were sold on open account. They were never paid for, and on December 5, 1975, an action for the price was brought. The defendant pleaded the three-year statute of limitations (12 Okla. Stat. § 95(2)), which allows three years to bring an action upon a contract, express or implied, that is not in writing. The plaintiff argued that § 2-725(1) of the Code, as enacted in Oklahoma, applied instead. While uniform Code § 2-725 provides for a four-year statute of limitations, Oklahoma amended § 2-725 to allow five years to sue for breach of a contract for a sale.

The court observed that none of the provisions of the general Oklahoma statute were expressly repealed when the state enacted the Code. Nonetheless, the court noted that the § 2-725 Official Comment stated a purpose to introduce a uniform statute of limitations for sales contracts in order to eliminate jurisdictional variations for businesses operating on a nationwide scale. It also noted the UCC is to be liberally construed and applied as stated in § 1-103(a). The court decided, based on the policy articulated in the Official Comment to that section, that the general statute of limitations should not apply and thus the action was timely brought. Further, the court did not allow Oklahoma's nonuniform amendment extending the limitations period from four to five years to destroy the overall goal of uniformity (although technically the reasoning of upholding a nonuniform amendment because of the goal of uniformity is nonsensical). This shows how minor tinkering potentially can impact larger goals, and other courts and legislatures have not always been as astute as the Oklahoma court in dealing with such deviations.

Numerous other decisions apply the purposes of the Code as a basis for finding that the Code's statute of limitations trumps other applicable statutes of limitations, on the grounds that applying the non-Code statute would impair uniformity. See, e.g., *Bort v. Sears, Roebuck & Co.,* 58 Misc. 2d 889, 296 N.Y.S.2d 739, 6 U.C.C. Rep. Serv. 146 (N.Y. City Ct. 1969) (refusing to apply negligence limitation to warranty action because to require plaintiffs to establish negligence would vitiate warranty and be contrary to policy of liberal construction to promote modernization of the law); *Johnson v. Hockessin Tractor, Inc.,* 420 A.2d 154, 29 U.C.C. Rep. Serv. 477 (Del. 1980) (refusing to apply two-year statute of limitations for action for personal injury on grounds it would be inconsistent with purpose of Code to simplify, clarify, and modernize the law); *Morton v. Texas Welding & Mfg. Co.,* 408 F. Supp. 7, 19 U.C.C. Rep. Serv. 137 (S.D. Tex. 1976) (same as preceding); and *United Crude Mktg. & Transp. Co. v. Robert Gordon Oil Co.,* 831 P.2d 659, 17 U.C.C. Rep. Serv. 2d 1172 (Okla. App. 1992) (refusing to apply three-year limitation for implied contract in action to recover overpayment under a purchase contract in order to achieve purpose of uniform treatment stated in Code); *Clancy Systems International, Inc. v. Salazar,* 177 P.3d 1235, 65 UCC Rep. Serv. 2d 137 (Colo.

2008) (when both the Code and common law would provide a means of recovery for the same loss, the common law should be preempted by the adoption of the UCC in the interest of furthering the Code's goal of uniformity).

In addition, numerous cases have applied the purpose provisions of the Code in relation to issues other than the statute of limitations. See, e.g., *Lige Dickson Co. v. Union Oil Co. of California*, 96 Wash. 2d 291, 635 P.2d 103, 32 U.C.C. Rep. Serv. 705 (1981) (purpose clause used in refusing to permit the doctrine of promissory estoppel to overcome a defense based on the statute of frauds in § 2-201); *Danning v. Bank of America N.T.S.A.,* 151 Cal. App. 3d 961, 199 Cal. Rptr. 163, 37 U.C.C. Rep. Serv. 1616 (1984) (court held purposes of the Code would be served by recognizing that the Code displaced the common law as to a bank's liability for negligence in dealing with its customer); and *Safe Deposit Bank & Trust Co. v. Berman,* 393 F.2d 401, 5 U.C.C. Rep. Serv. 1 (1st Cir. 1968) (applying Massachusetts law) (court held that a provision of the Code must be read in light of the purposes and policies stated in what is now § 1-103(a).

The purpose of uniformity also means that any court deciding a Code case must consider cases from other jurisdictions as precedent unless the case is clearly contrary to the Code or Official Comments. For example, in *Northrop Corp. v. Litronic Industries*, 29 F.3d 1173, 24 U.C.C. Rep. Serv. 2d 407 (7th Cir. 1994) (applying Illinois law), the federal court sitting in diversity had to decide a UCC issue arising under Illinois law that had not been addressed by the courts of that state. Holding his nose because he did not agree with the majority rule, Judge Posner stated:

> Because Illinois in other UCC cases has tended to adopt majority rules, e.g., *Rebaque v. Forsythe Racing, Inc.*, 134 Ill. App. 3d 778, 89 Ill. Dec. 595, 598, 480 N.E.2d 1338, 1341 (1985), and because the interest in the uniform nationwide application of the Code—an interest asserted in the Code itself

(see [§ 1-103(a)(3)])—argues for nudging majority
views, even if imperfect (but not downright bad),
toward unanimity, we start with a presumption that
Illinois, whose position we are trying to predict,
would adopt the majority view. We do not find the
presumption rebutted.

For a case in which a jurisdiction where the point was unde-
cided used a case from another jurisdiction to decide a point, see
Reynolds-Wilson Lumber Co. v. Peoples Nat'l Bank, 699 P.2d
146 (Okla. 1985), and *Nat'l Environmental Serv. Co. v. Ronan
Eng'g Co.,* 256 F.3d 995, 45 UCC Rep. Serv. 2d 430 (10th Cir.
2001) (applying Oklahoma law). See also *Husker News Co. v.
Mahaska State Bank,* 460 N.W.2d 476, 13 U.C.C. Rep. Serv. 2d
46 (Iowa 1990) and *Hollywood v. First Nat'l Bank of Palmerton,*
859 A.2d 472, 54 UCC Rep. Serv. 2d 343 (Pa. Super. 2004),
(refusing to apply discovery rule to a conversion action given
that other states are nearly unanimous in their refusal to apply
the doctrine); *Yamaha Motor Corp., U.S.A. v. Tri-City Motors
& Sports, Inc.,* 171 Mich. App. 260, 429 N.W.2d 871, 7 U.C.C.
Rep. Serv. 2d 1190 (1988) (where uniform laws such as the UCC
have been adopted by several states, the courts of one state may
refer to decisions from another state and construe the statutes in
accordance with the construction given by that state); *Brewster of
Lynchburg, Inc. v. Dial Corp.,* 33 F.3d 355, 24 U.C.C. Rep. Serv.
2d 738 (4th Cir. 1994) (applying Arizona law) (Arizona courts
frequently resort to case law from other jurisdictions to interpret
statutes modeled after the UCC); and *Morris v. People's Bank
and Trust Co. of Natchitoches,* 580 So. 2d 1037, 15 U.C.C. Rep.
Serv. 2d 575 (La. App. 1991) (where no Louisiana law interpreting
§ 8-319 exists, the court will look to the law of other jurisdictions
in an effort to harmonize commercial law among the states). In
theory, then, a court should find sound case authority from another
jurisdiction to be more persuasive than its own precedents.

D. Expansion to Non-Code Transactions

The idea of employing the purposes of the Code to resolve issues arising outside the Code involves an even broader concept. Numerous courts have applied provisions of the Code by extension or analogy to transactions not literally covered by the Code at that time. See, e.g., *All States Leasing Co. v. Bass,* 96 Idaho 873, 538 P.2d 1177, 17 U.C.C. Rep. Serv. 933 (1975) (leases); *Division of Triple T Service, Inc. v. Mobil Oil Corp.,* 60 Misc. 2d 720, 304 N.Y.S.2d 191, 6 U.C.C. Rep. Serv. 1011 (N.Y. Sup. Ct. 1969), *aff'd without opinion,* 311 N.Y.S.2d 961 (App. Div. 1970) (franchise and distributorship agreement); and *Custom Communications Eng'g, Inc. v. E.F. Johnson Co.,* 269 N.J. Super. 531, 636 A.2d 80, 22 U.C.C. Rep. Serv. 2d 971 (1993) (dealership or distributorship agreement). The Pennsylvania Supreme Court also applied the policy behind § 2A-506 in a case even though Pennsylvania had yet to adopt Article 2A. See *Cucchi v. Rollins Protective Servs.,* 524 Pa. 514, 574 A.2d 565, 11 U.C.C. Rep. Serv. 2d 737 (1990). See also *Norcon Power Partners, L.P. v. Niagara Mohawk Power Corp.*, 92 N.Y.2d 458, 705 N.E.2d 656, 682 N.Y.S.2d 664, 37 UCC Rep. Serv. 2d 323 (N.Y. 1998) (applying UCC § 2-609 to the sale of electricity).

This approach to Code jurisprudence can frequently be seen in the case of software. The Prefatory Note to the Uniform Computer Information Transactions Act (UCITA) states:

> Just as a body of law based on images of the sale of horses was not relevant a half century ago to sales of manufactured goods, so today a body of law [Article 2] based on images of the sale of manufactured goods ill fits licenses and other transactions in computer information.

Nevertheless, while UCITA was enacted in only two states and then withdrawn by the ULC and the ALI, the body of principles in the Code is frequently seen as relevant to transactions in computer information.

In 2009, the ALI adopted the *Principles of the Law of Software Contracts*. Unlike the ALI's Restatements, which are descriptive in nature, *Principles* is prescriptive, promulgating rules that the authors believe should be applied in this area of law. Many of the rules are analogous to Code rules as found in Article 2. The Summary Overview to each topic and the Comment to each Principle provide an invaluable guide to the practitioner who is attempting to fashion a rule in a case involving software.

Of course, the process of using Code rules by analogy entails the risk that a provision or concept may be inappropriately applied considering the different subject matter of the non-Code-governed transaction and differences in practice, among other things. For example, courts that drew from UCC Articles 3 and 4 for rules to govern funds transfers before Article 4A was prepared may have reached some inappropriate conclusions or results. Thus, the Official Comment to § 4A-305 notes, concerning the pre-Article 4A case of *Evra Corp. v. Swiss Bank Corp.,* 673 F.2d 951 (7th Cir. 1982) (applying Illinois law): "If *Evra* means that consequential damages can be imposed if the culpable bank has notice of particular circumstances giving rise to the damages, it does not provide an acceptable solution to the problem of bank liability for consequential damages." In short, while the overall concept is sound, the proper result is largely a product of care in the implementation of the concept.

CODE AND NON-CODE LAW
§ 1-103(b)

§ 1-103. Construction of [Uniform Commercial Code] to Promote Its Purposes and Policies; Applicability of Supplemental Principles of Law.

(b)   Unless displaced by the particular provisions of [the Uniform Commercial Code], the principles of law and equity, including the law merchant and the law relative to capacity to contract, principal and agent, estoppel, fraud, misrepresentation, duress, coercion, mistake, bankruptcy, and other validating or invalidating cause supplement its provisions.

A. The Relationship of the Code to Federal Law

Because of constitutional principles of preemption, federal law, where applicable, including international conventions adopted by the United States, will control over the Code. Indeed, if the rights of the United States or an instrumentality of the United States are involved, the Code, as state law, cannot govern. But where there is no federal statute or regulation, the Code may be adopted as the federal rule of decision, that is, as a rule of federal common law. See *United States v. Smith,* 832 F.2d 774, 4 U.C.C. Rep. Serv. 2d 1001 (2nd Cir. 1987) (applying New York law), and *United States v. Conrad Publ. Co.,* 589 F.2d 949, 25 U.C.C. Rep. Serv. 857 (8th Cir. 1978) (applying North Dakota law). As to when circumstances are appropriate, see, e.g., *United States v. Kimbell Foods, Inc.,* 440 U.S. 715, 26 U.C.C. Rep. Serv. 1 (1979) (applying Texas law).

B. Supplementation

Section 1-103(b) makes supplementary principles of law applicable to Code issues. Thus, other law, both federal and state, and both statutory and common law, may supplement the Code. However, the common law does not apply when it has been displaced by a Code provision. An Official Comment to former § 1-103 stated that other law would supplement the Code unless it is "explicitly displaced" by a Code provision. Official Comment 2 corrects that view, stating:The 'explicitly displaced' language of that Comment did not accurately reflect the proper scope of Uniform Commercial Code preemption, which extends to displacement of other law that is inconsistent with the purposes and policies of the Uniform Commercial Code, as well as with its text.

For example, in *Hitachi Electronic Devices (USA), Inc. v. Platinum Technologies, Inc.,* 366 S.C. 163, 621 S.E.2d 38, 57 U.C.C. Rep. Serv. 2d 883 (2005), the buyer failed to give the seller adequate notice of breach of warranty under § 2-607(3). The trial court nevertheless held that while this failure barred it from pursuing Code remedies, the buyer was not barred from pursuing common law remedies. The appellate court reversed, holding that the "comprehensive system of remedies for breach of warranty" in the Code was intended to displace the common law.

On occasion, a Code provision explicitly directs that other law may override a Code provision. For example, § 2-102 states in part:

> Nor does this Article impair or repeal any statute regulating sales to consumers, farmers or other specified classes of buyers.

Examples of such statutes include the federal Magnuson Moss Warranty Act, 15 U.S.C. §§ 2301-2312, and state Consumer Protection Acts. Similarly, § 9-201(b) and (c) defer to special laws that establish rules for consumers and other specified classes of persons. Examples include the Food Security Act, 7 U.S.C. § 1631, and the Packers and Stockyards Act, 7 U.S.C. § 196.

Section 3-302(g) subordinates holder-in-due-course status under the Code to any law limiting that status in particular classes of transactions, such as a consumer transaction. An example of such a law is the Federal Trade Commission holder-in-Due-Course regulations, 16 C.F.R. Part 433. Section 8-509(a) allows compliance with another statute, regulation, or rule in certain circumstances to satisfy a duty imposed by §§ 8-504 through 8-508. In short, a Code transaction, especially one involving a consumer, often involves the application of other law.

Resort to non-Code law often is necessary to implement the Code fully. For example, § 9-203(b)(3)(A) requires that a security agreement be authenticated, but who has authority to authenticate is not determined by the Code. Instead, it is determined by the law of agency that supplements it. Similarly, defenses to contract formation, such as lack of capacity, fraud, or mistake, are rarely mentioned in Articles 2, 2A, or 9, but they must be applied to determine whether an enforceable contract for sale, lease, or security agreement has been formed.

An early case recognizing the synergies between Code and non-Code law is *French Lumber Co. v. Commercial Realty & Finance Co.*, 346 Mass. 716, 195 N.E.2d 507, 2 U.C.C. Rep. Serv. 3 (1964). In that case, French purchased a car and Ware financed it, taking and perfecting a security interest by filing. Later French obtained a loan on the equity in the car from Commercial, which got a second security interest, also perfected by filing. Finally, Associates loaned French money to pay off Ware and took a third security interest, perfected by filing, to secure the debt. French defaulted, and there was a dispute as to who had the prior security interest, Commercial or Associates. Under what is now § 9-322(a)(1), Commercial would have prevailed since it was first to file or perfect. The court held, however, that pursuant to what is now § 1-103(b), because Associates was subrogated to Ware's old interest, its interest was perfected by the original filing by Ware, and Associates thus had first priority. The equitable principle of subrogation was thus held not displaced by the Article 9 priority rules in order to prevent unjust enrichment.

C. Supplementation or Displacement

The hard question is whether a legal principle contained in law outside the Code is supplementary or has been displaced. In former Article 1, § 1-102(1) and (2) contained the Code purposes and policies, while former § 1-103 contained the rule on supplementation. This arrangement seemed to signal that law outside the Code should be utilized unless a particular Code section provided the necessary rule. Revised § 1-103, by combining former § 1-102(1) and (2) and former § 1-103 into one section, may seek to expose the tension and thus lead courts to balance the two mandates in a more appropriate way as the circumstances indicate. One might say that process involves determining not just whether one can find a particular governing Code section, but also whether application of the outside rule would substantially impair a fundamental objective involved in the Code section or in a larger Code plan. *French Lumber Company* might well be decided differently today under this analysis, for a court might determine that application of the equitable doctrine of subrogation would impair the certainty the Code seeks for resolving priority among secured parties.

For example, in *Daniels-Sheridan Federal Credit Union v. Ballenger*, 2001 MT 235, 36 P.3d 397 (2001), plaintiff credit union had a security interest in cattle owned by Leland. When Leland defaulted, the credit union sought to foreclose on the cattle, which included cattle sold by one Smith to Leland on credit. Smith did not have a security interest, but claimed that he had an "equitable interest" in the cattle. The trial court held that it would result in unjust enrichment to allow the credit union to recover cattle delivered by Smith to Leland. The Montana Supreme Court reversed, holding that while equitable principles can supplement the Code, in this case they had been displaced by the priority rules expressly provided in the UCC.

A representative sampling of cases decided under former § 1-103 includes *S. S. Kresge Co. v. Port of Longview,* 18 Wash. App. 805, 573 P.2d 1336, 23 U.C.C. Rep. Serv. 431 (1977) (court determined that § 7-204, which codifies the obligation of a warehouse to exercise ordinary care, is supplemented by common law rules pertaining to bailments for mutual benefit, such as the rule creating a presumption of negligence when property is delivered to a bailee in good condition and is lost or damaged while in the bailee's possession); *Harney-Morgan Chevrolet Olds Co. v. Rabin,* 118 Ill. App. 3d 602, 455 N.E.2d 130, 37 U.C.C. Rep. Serv. 50 (1983) (court held that the doctrine of mistake was available to supplement the Code); *Gen. Ins. Co. of America v. Lowry,* 570 F.2d 120, 23 U.C.C. Rep. Serv. 1058 (6th Cir. 1978) (applying Ohio law) (court held that the priority provisions of Article 9 did not prevent the imposition of an equitable lien under the unusual facts present in that case involving a person promoting his/her own interest to the detriment of another to whom a duty of good faith was owed); *United Bank of Arizona v. Mesa N.O. Nelson Co., Inc.,* 121 Ariz. 438, 590 P.2d 1384, 25 U.C.C. Rep. Serv. 1113 (1979) (court suggested that the doctrines of ratification and estoppel were consistent with the Code allocation of fraud losses); and *Lund v. Chemical Bank,* 797 F. Supp. 259, 19 U.C.C. Rep. Serv. 2d 151 (S.D.N.Y. 1992) (court concluded, as have other courts, that a drawee sued by a payee of a check whose indorsement was forged is not precluded, by the Code plan for fraud loss allocation, from raising an unjust enrichment defense to the extent of any previous recovery of part of the loss by the payee, such as from the forger).

On this last point, see also *True v. Fleet Bank,* 138 N.H. 679, 645 A.2d 671, 24 U.C.C. Rep. Serv. 2d 598 (1994) (taking perhaps an unduly restrictive view).

On the other hand, the Code rule was held to displace other law in *Flavor-lnn, Inc. v. NCNB Nat'l Bank of South Carolina,* 309 S.C. 508, 424 S.E.2d 534, 19 U.C.C. Rep. Serv. 2d 1116 (1992) (court ruled that an action for conversion of the instrument recognized by the Code and arising from a depository bank's payment or acceptance for deposit of checks on unauthorized indorsements supplanted any action of the payee in negligence) and *Trinidad Bean & Elevator Co. v. Frosh,* 1 Neb, App. 281, 494 N.W.2d 347, 20 U.C.C. Rep. Serv. 2d 462 (1992) (on facts present in the case, court determined it was an error to have given an instruction on mitigation of damages even though in most cases courts have concluded that the doctrine requiring mitigation of damages is applicable in Code cases). Clearly, one has to have a keen understanding of the purposes and policies of the Code to address the question of displacement, and even then the answer is best learned after litigation and is not always discernible before the issue is put into contention.

The conflict between supplementation and displacement is well-illustrated by a comparison between the case of *Ninth District Production Credit Ass'n v. Ed Duggan, Inc.,* 821 P.2d 788, 16 U.C.C. Rep. Serv. 2d 853 (Colo. 1991) and *Knox v. Phoenix Leasing Inc.,* 29 Cal. App. 4th 1357, 35 Cal. Rptr. 2d 141, 24 U.C.C. Rep. Serv. 2d 1049 (Ct. App. 1994). In *Ed Duggan,* the court applied the doctrine of unjust enrichment against a secured creditor whose collateral value was enhanced by the unsecured creditor's action in circumstances where the secured creditor was perceived to have initiated or encouraged transactions between the debtor and the unsecured creditor that benefited the secured creditor. The court applied the doctrine in the case even though it upset the order of priorities established under Article 9. The case is similar in many ways to *French Lumber Company,* which the court cited, and also may be consistent with the imposition of an equitable lien, as the court did in *Lowry.*

In contrast, the court in *Knox* as a general policy expressed a preference for the Code scheme to displace the ability of an unsecured creditor to obtain restitution from a protected secured creditor because the Code established a predictable system of creditor priorities. Even so, the *Knox* court agreed with *Ed Duggan* that it might award restitution in a case involving something more than mere benefit realized by the secured creditor. That "something more" might arise where the secured creditor's conduct promoted the transaction that benefited it, or where the unsecured creditor provided goods or services necessary to preserve the collateral.

In the end, determining what law outside the Code is supplementary and what is displaced cannot, and should not, be an exact science. Like the doctrine of unconscionability under §§ 2-302 and 2A-108, content for the concept is built up in the case law over the years. The cases sooner or later may build a pattern that assists in some degree of predictability. For example, a principle that may be derived from *French Lumber Company, Ed Duggan, Lowry,* and *Knox* is that conduct by a party that benefits that party at the expense of another under circumstances that offend good business morality is unlikely to be tolerated. See, e.g., § 9-328 Official Comment 8.

D. Predictability

With the concept of the tension between supplementation and displacement in mind, it may be possible to predict results in variable fact patterns. To illustrate, suppose an Article 2 buyer is deprived of the benefit of the contract before the goods are identified to the contract by the action of a third party that amounts to tortious interference with contract. There is no remedy against the third party under § 2-722 because that provision only awards status to sue for actionable injury with respect to goods identified to the contract. But can it be said that § 2-722 is exclusive and any other theory of remedy is displaced? Probably not, and the court in *In re Quality Processing, Inc.,* 9 F.3d 1360, 22 U.C.C. Rep. Serv. 2d 525 (8th Cir. 1993) (applying Nebraska law) agreed. Results consistent with this analysis were also reached in *Deluxe Sales & Service, Inc. v. Hyundai Engineering & Const. Co., Ltd.,* 254 N.J. Super. 370, 603 A.2d 552, 18 U.C.C. Rep. Serv. 2d 1145 (1992) (court refused relief when the buyer had not intentionally lulled the seller into believing payment was forthcoming) and *Hanna v. First Nat'l Bank of Rochester,* 159 Misc. 2d 1, 602 N.Y.S.2d 762, 23 U.C.C. Rep. Serv. 2d 142 (1993) (court refused to allow a payee recovery against the bank which delayed action on the check when the payee was aware that, absent a mistake, the check would be dishonored).

Another principle derived from *French Lumber Company* and like cases may be that a windfall to a third party at the expense of a party will not be tolerated if the third party is not prejudiced by prevention of the windfall. This concept should have allowed prediction of the results in *Page v. Dobbs Mobile Bay, Inc.,* 599 So. 2d 38, 18 U.C.C. Rep. Serv. 2d 720 (Ala. App. 1992) (court reduced the buyers' recovery to reflect their continued beneficial use of a defective van after the buyer rejected it) and *Bombardier Capital, Inc. v. Key Bank of Maine,* 639 A.2d 1065, 24 U.C.C. Rep. Serv. 2d 647 (Me. 1994) (court allowed the use of equitable tracing with respect to funds in a commingled account to identify a secured party's proceeds so the security interest was not lost to a setoff by the bank in which the account was held).

However, these types of cases also must carefully consider the impact of the decision on Code policies such as predictability and certainty. Doing justice between the parties may cause unpredictability with respect to other transactions, and cases like *French Lumber Company* may be criticized as not adequately considering this risk. In this view, as suggested, § 1-103's sharper focus may result in a different outcome. Nonetheless, the risk should not be overstated because the decisions all emphasize factual differences and thus afford an opportunity to cabin the actual result. Therefore, as in the case of the wild card of unconscionability or jury determinations of holding in due course, precedential value (or, conversely, damage to a general Code policy) is heavily dependent on factual distinctions. This concept is illustrated by the case of *In re Rainbow Mfg. Co.,* 150 B.R. 857, 22 U.C.C. Rep. Serv. 2d 352 (M.D. Ga. 1993), in which the court refused to penalize a secured creditor for a mistake in compliance in the midst of what it characterized as a changing legal landscape and conflicting statutes. The promotion of equity at the expense of certainty in this case is virtually risk free as it is unlikely that the confusion in the Georgia law that caused the problem in the case will ever be replicated exactly.

For a discussion in greater depth, see Sarah Howard Jenkins, *Preemption & Supplementation Under Revised § 1-103: The Role of Common Law & Equity in the New U.C.C.,* 54 SMU L. Rev. 495 (2001). The author points out that of the cases litigated under former § 1-103, three classes are now resolved by particular provisions of the Code: applicability of conversion (§ 3-420), ability to obtain restitution (§ 3-418), and applicability of accord and satisfaction (former § 1-207(b)—now § 1-308—and § 3-311). This, the author concludes, only leaves the issue of applicability of the doctrines of waiver and estoppel. As to those doctrines, the author postulates that § 1-103 now compels the conclusion that the paramount rule of construction is preemption by the Code, and that preemption extends to the displacement of any law that is inconsistent with the Code's express terms or its purposes and policies. That is, supplementation no longer stands on an equal footing with the purposes and policies of the Code but is one of several considerations to be balanced rather than separately accommodated. Nonetheless, the original purpose of what is now § 1-103(b)—to prevent the Code sections from operating mechanically—should also be accommodated because the appropriate use of supplemental principles avoids the need for judicial manipulation, which can lead to more uncertainty than does such accommodation.

CHAPTER

6

CONSTRUCTION AGAINST IMPLIED REPEAL § 1-104

§ 1-104. Construction Against Implied Repeal.

[The Uniform Commercial Code] being a general act intended as a unified coverage of its subject matter, no part of it shall be deemed to be impliedly repealed by subsequent legislation if such construction can reasonably be avoided.

Under § 1-104, subsequent legislation that does not expressly repeal the Code should not be interpreted as impliedly repealing it. One interesting application of this principle occurred in *Brown v. Yousif,* 198 Mich. App. 667, 499 N.W.2d 446, 20 U.C.C. Rep. Serv. 2d 1074 (1993), *aff'd on other grounds,* 445 Mich. 222, 517 N.W.2d 727, 24 U.C.C. Rep. Serv. 2d 275 (1994), in which the court held that the Michigan Liquor Control Commission did not have authority to repeal or amend Article 9 of the Code by determining that a security interest could not be created in a liquor license.

CHAPTER

7

§ 1-105. Severability.

If any provision or clause of [the Uniform Commercial Code] or its application to any person or circumstance is held invalid, the invalidity does not affect other provisions or applications of [the Uniform Commercial Code] which can be given effect without the invalid provision or application, and to this end the provisions of [the Uniform Commercial Code] are severable.

Section 1-105 in a sense reinforces the concept, which was emphasized in the discussion of § 1-103, that the Code is an integrated statute. The section does so by seeking to preserve the validity of the balance of the Code even if one or more of its provisions or the application of those provisions should be held invalid. To that end, it provides that the provisions of the Code are severable.

Accordingly, when the title of the bill did not mention that § 2-725 (the Article 2 statute of limitations) changed the previous statutes of limitations for sales contracts—thus contravening the provisions of the Maryland Constitution which require that every law enacted embrace one subject matter that shall be described in the title—the failure did not render the Code as enacted unconstitutional. *Madison Nat'l Bank v. Newrath,* 261 Md. 321, 275 A.2d 495, 8 U.C.C. Rep. Serv. 1153 (1971).

CHAPTER

8

USE OF SINGULAR AND PLURAL; GENDER § 1-106

---

§ 1-106. Use of Singular and Plural; Gender.

In [the Uniform Commercial Code], unless the statutory context otherwise requires:

(1) words in the singular number include the plural, and those in the plural include the singular; and

(2) words of any gender also refer to any other gender.

Section 1-106 is probably unnecessary, as more general acts regarding the construction of statutes and rules in the enacting jurisdiction likely cover the matters dealt with in this section. Section 1-106(2) has an increasingly smaller role to play in the Code, as revisions are now written in gender-neutral language. For example, former § 1-208 was revised to improve grammar and eliminate sexist language. It is now found as follows in § 1-309 (the strikethroughs represent deleted words and the underscores represent added words):

A term providing that one party or ~~his~~ that party's successor in interest may accelerate payment or performance or require collateral or additional collateral "at will" or "when ~~he~~ the party deems ~~himself~~ itself insecure" or ~~in~~ words of similar import, ~~shall be construed to~~ means that ~~he~~ the party ~~shall have~~ has power to do so only if ~~he~~ that party in good faith believes that the prospect of payment or performance is impaired.

CHAPTER

9

SECTION CAPTIONS
§ 1-107

§ 1-107. Section Captions.

Section captions are part of [the Uniform Commercial Code].

The Code provision on captions differs from the general rule. A state legislature generally enacts the text of a law without section captions, which are then added by an administrative agency. Because they are not promulgated by the legislature, the section captions do not have the force of law.

The UCC, on the other hand, comes pre-packaged with section captions and is enacted *in toto*, captions and all, by the legislature. Thus, the UCC is the exception to the general rule that section captions are not part of the statute.

An exception to the exception is the subsection headings added for convenience in Revised Article 9. These are found in brackets in the uniform version, indicating their limbo-like status—each jurisdiction must determine whether to adopt them. As noted in comment 3 to § 9-101:

This Article also includes headings for the subsections as an aid to readers. Unlike section captions, which are part of the UCC, see Section 1-109 [revised § 1-107], subsection headings are not a part of the official text itself and have not been approved by the sponsors. Each jurisdiction in which this Article is introduced may consider whether to adopt the headings as a part of the statute and whether to adopt a provision clarifying the effect, if any, to be given to the headings.

A problem in the subsection headings was discussed in a footnote in *In re Schwalb*, 347 B.R. 726 (D. Nev. 2006). Judge Markell raised the issue of whether § 9-625(c) penalties are available only in a "consumer-goods transaction," as provided in the subsection heading, even though the text of the subsection itself refers to the broader transaction in which "the collateral is consumer goods." The judge noted that the argument based on the subsection headings is unavailing because the subsection headings are not part of the Code—and in any event Nevada did not enact § 1-107. The error in the subsection heading to § 9-625 has been corrected in Amended Article 9.

California, Connecticut, Indiana, Louisiana, and Tennessee also omitted § 1-107 when enacting Revised Article 1; Oregon enacted a nonuniform version of § 1-107 that specifically states that captions are not part of the law.

There are a few cases in which section captions have been used for purposes of interpretation. The courts seem to have gotten it right by using the text of the caption to construe the meaning of the provision. In *Philbin v. Matanuska-Susitna Borough*, 991 P.2d 1263 (Alaska 1999), the issue concerned the interpretation of former § 1-107, now revised § 1-306. The plaintiff argued that a release was not effective because it was made *before* the breach and, although the text is silent on when the release has to be made, the caption refers to "Waiver or Renunciation of Claim or Right *After* Breach." The court agreed with this interpretation.

In *Bethlehem Steel Corp. v. Litton Indus., Inc.*, 468 A.2d 748 (Pa. Super. Ct. 1983), the court's conclusion that Article 2 applied to a transaction even though the buyer had only an option to order goods was buttressed by the fact that the caption to § 2-311 refers to "Options and Cooperation Respecting Performance."

The revision of Article 1 and the now withdrawn amendments to Article 2 did not change either of the captions involved in these cases. By contrast, the following Article 9 cases all arose under former Article 9 and the ambiguities that were raised have all been resolved in Revised Article 9.

In *First Nat'l Bank & Trust Co. of Norman, Oklahoma v. Jim Payne Pontiac GMC, Inc.*, 1976 WL 23704 (Okla. Ct. App. 1976), a case decided under the pre-1972 version of Article 9, an automobile was sold by an owner in Texas, a certificate-of-title state, to a buyer in Oklahoma, which at the time was not a certificate-of-title state. The bank had perfected its interest in the Oklahoma debtor's property by filing. The unpaid seller claimed that the bank's security interest was not perfected because § 9-103 provided in pertinent part that "if personal property is covered by a certificate of title issued under a statute of this state or any other jurisdiction which requires indication on a certificate of title of any security interest in the property as a condition of perfection, then the perfection is governed by the law of the jurisdiction which issued the certificate." If read literally, perfection would be governed by Texas law, which required notation on the certificate of title. But the court pointed out that the caption to § 9-103 provided: "Accounts, Contract Rights, General Intangibles and Equipment Relating to Another Jurisdiction; and Incoming Goods Already Subject to a Security Interest." Since the automobile was not already subject to a security interest in Texas, the rule did not apply. No such ambiguity exists in Revised Article 9.

In *In re San Juan Packers, Inc.*, 696 F.2d 707 (9th Cir. 1983) (applying Washington law), a secured party argued that a security interest did not remain attached to goods that were commingled but not processed. This argument was based on the caption to pre-1972 § 9-315, which read, "Priority When Goods Are Commingled or Processed," although the *or* in that caption made clear that the goods do not need to be processed for the section to apply. This rule is now found in revised § 9-336, which is simply captioned "Commingled Goods" and which, unlike its predecessor, contains a definition of *commingled goods*.

In *Medi-fi Two Inc. v. Riordan*, 390 N.E.2d 1 (Ill. Ct. App. 1979), an accounts financier claimed that a debtor was liable to it for a "deficiency" in payments from a third-party. The financier cited to the rule of former § 9-504(2), which provided that "the debtor is liable for any deficiency." However, the court cited the caption to § 9-504, which stated, "Secured Party's Right to Dispose of Collateral After Default; Effect of Disposition," to indicate that the rule applied only when there was a disposition of the collateral after default. Revised § 9-615 makes clear that the deficiency rules apply following a disposition of collateral and revised § 9-608(a)(4) and (b) specify when a debtor is liable for a deficiency after collection.

In *Executive Bank of Ft. Lauderdale v. Tighe*, 429 N.E.2d 1054 (N.Y. 1981), the issue was whether the bank had to give notice of a bankruptcy sale. The governing law, former § 9-504(3), provided that the secured party must give the debtor notice of a sale. But the court held that because the caption refers to "Secured Party's Right to Dispose of Collateral After Default," the notice provision applies only when the secured party is conducting the sale. This provision is clarified in revised § 9-611(b), which provides that "a secured party that disposes of collateral under Section 9-610 shall send ... notification of disposition."

In *In re Fullop*, 133 B.R. 627, 16 U.C.C. Rep. Serv. 2d 820 (S.D. Ill. 1991), *mod., and as mod., aff'd* 21 U.C.C. Rep. Serv. 2d 757, the trustee argued that because the heading of former § 9-103 was "Perfection of Security Interests in Multiple State Transactions," subsection (5), which dealt with the perfection of a security interest in minerals, applied only to cases involving interstate transactions. The court rejected the trustee's argument, holding that "although a court may consider the title or heading of a statute as an aid to determining the legislative intent where the language of the statute is obscure or ambiguous, 'the plain meaning of the substantive provisions of the section cannot be limited by its heading.'" [Citations omitted.]

CHAPTER
10

RELATION TO FEDERAL E-SIGN ACT
§ 1-108

§ 1-108. Relation to Electronic Signatures in Global and National Commerce Act.

This article modifies, limits, and supersedes the federal Electronic Signatures in Global and National Commerce Act, 15 U.S.C. Section 7001 *et seq.*, except that nothing in this article modifies, limits, or supersedes Section 7001(c) of that Act or authorizes electronic delivery of any of the notices described in Section 7003(b) of that Act.

A. Background; Federal E-Sign Legislation

In 2000, Congress enacted and the President signed the Electronic Signatures in Global and National Commerce Act (E-Sign), 15 U.S.C. § 7001 *et seq.* The purpose of the act is to override unnecessary signature and writing requirements in federal and state law that constitute an impediment to the development of electronic commerce. Section 7001(a) of the act provides:

> Notwithstanding any statute, regulation, or other rule of law (other than this subchapter and subchapter II of this chapter), with respect to any transaction in or affecting interstate or foreign commerce—
>
> > (1) a signature, contract, or other record relating to such transaction may not be denied legal effect, validity, or enforceability solely because it is in electronic form; and
> >
> > (2) a contract relating to such transaction may not be denied legal effect, validity, or enforceability solely because an electronic signature or electronic record was used in its formation.

This federal legislation occurred even though at the same time the Uniform Electronic Transactions Act (UETA), a uniform state law that accomplished the same goals as the federal act but was more comprehensive, was receiving widespread enactment in the states. An issue, therefore, is the appropriate relationship between the two statutes in states that have enacted UETA. On that issue, see Shea Meehan and D. Benjamin Beard, *What Hath Congress Wrought: E-Sign, the UETA, and the Question of Preemption*, 37 Idaho L. Rev. 389 (2001).

B. Reconciling E-Sign and UETA

Congress had anticipated UETA; indeed, Congress had lifted large segments from it for the federal statute. Section 7003(a)(3) of the federal act also provides:

> The provisions of Section 7001 of this title shall not apply to a contract or other record to the extent it is governed by— ...
>
> > (3) the Uniform Commercial Code, as in effect in any State, other than Sections 1–107

[Revised § 1-306] and 1–206 [deleted from Revised Article 1] and Articles 2 and 2A.

Presumably, then, Article 1 is exempt from the federal statute, except for § 1-306. That provision, discussed in Chapter 19, was revised to conform to E-Sign. The Official Comment notes as part of the "Changes from former law:"

> Second, the revised section reflects develop-ments in electronic commerce by providing for memorialization in an authenticated record. In this context, a party may "authenticate" a record by (i) signing a record that is a writing or (ii) attaching to or logically associating with a record that is not a writing an electronic sound, symbol or process with the present intent to adopt or accept the record. See Sections 1-201(b)(37) and 9-102(a)(7).

Even if § 1-306 had not been revised to conform to E-Sign, § 7002(a) of E-Sign provides that a state statute may modify, limit, or supersede the provisions of § 7001 of E-Sign with respect to state law if the statute meets certain criteria. The first clause of § 1-108 is designed to take advantage of this provision of E-Sign, perhaps in part out of an abundance of caution, given the almost complete exemption for Article 1 in § 7003(a)(3). The Official Comment explains that Article 1 satisfies these criteria:

> The federal Electronic Signatures in Global and National Commerce Act, 15 U.S.C. Section 7001 *et seq.*, became effective in 2000. Section 102(a) of that Act provides that a State statute may modify, limit, or supersede the provisions of Section 101 of that Act with respect to state law if such statute, *inter alia*, specifies the alternative procedures or requirements for the use or acceptance (or both) of electronic records or electronic signatures to

establish the legal effect, validity, or enforceability
of contracts or other records, and (i) such alternative procedures or requirements are consistent with
Titles I and II of that Act, (ii) such alternative procedures or requirements do not require, or accord
greater legal status or effect to, the implementation
or application of a specific technology or technical
specification for performing the functions of creating, storing, generating, receiving, communicating,
or authenticating electronic records or electronic
signatures; and (iii) if enacted or adopted after the
date of the enactment of that Act, makes specific
reference to that Act. Article 1 fulfills the first two
of those three criteria; this Section fulfills the third
criterion listed above.

Section 1-108 has another purpose, as set forth in the exception
that follows the initial clause, of retaining the consumer protection
provisions of E-Sign. The UETA contains substantial protections
for consumers. For example, electronic use must be consensual
(§ 5(b)), consumers must be able to receive and retain the electronic record (§ 8(a)), and any specific legal delivery requirements
must be met in electronic form (§ 8(b)). Nonetheless, § 7001(c)
of E-Sign provides for more elaborate consumer consent to electronic records provisions. For additional information, see Robert
A. Wittie and Jane K. Winn, *Electronic Records and Signatures
under the Federal E-Sign Legislation and the UETA*, 56 Bus. Law.
293 (Nov. 2000).

Section 7003(b) further provides that § 7001 does not apply
to documents involved in court proceedings and a variety of
notices, such as a cancellation or termination of utility services.
The Article 1 drafting committee made a decision that otherwise applicable state laws would not supersede these greater
protections found in E-Sign. Accordingly, § 1-108 goes on to
state that "nothing in this article modifies, limits, or supersedes

Section 7001(c) of that Act or authorizes electronic delivery of any of the notices described in Section 7003(b) of that Act."

Thus, with one exception, E-Sign does not apply to Article 1 for two reasons: 1) E-Sign expressly states that it does not apply to Article 1, except for § 1-306, which conforms to E-Sign, and 2) § 1-108, in conformity with the requirements of E-Sign, provides that Article 1 supersedes E-Sign. The exception is for the more extensive consumer consent and notice provisions of E-Sign that are applicable to the extent Article 1 applies to a transaction.

CHAPTER

11

GENERAL DEFINITIONS
§§ 1-201 THROUGH 1-204

---

§ 1-201. General Definitions.

(a)   Unless the context otherwise requires, words or phrases defined in this section, or in the additional definitions contained in other articles of [the Uniform Commercial Code] that apply to particular articles or parts thereof, have the meanings stated.

(b)   Subject to definitions contained in other articles of [the Uniform Commercial Code] that apply to particular articles or parts thereof:

(1)   "Action", in the sense of a judicial proceeding, includes recoupment, counterclaim, setoff, suit in equity, and any other proceeding in which rights are determined.

(2)   "Aggrieved party" means a party entitled to pursue a remedy.

(3)   "Agreement", as distinguished from "contract", means the bargain of the parties in fact, as found in their language or inferred from other circumstances, including course of

performance, course of dealing, or usage of trade as provided in Section 1-303.

(4) "Bank" means a person engaged in the business of banking and includes a savings bank, savings and loan association, credit union, and trust company.

(5) "Bearer" means a person in control of a negotiable electronic document of title or a person in possession of a negotiable instrument, negotiable tangible document of title, or certificated security that is payable to bearer or indorsed in blank.

(6) "Bill of lading" means a document of title evidencing the receipt of goods for shipment issued by a person engaged in the business of directly or indirectly transporting or forwarding goods. The term does not include a warehouse receipt.

(7) "Branch" includes a separately incorporated foreign branch of a bank.

(8) "Burden of establishing" a fact means the burden of persuading the trier of fact that the existence of the fact is more probable than its nonexistence.

(9) "Buyer in ordinary course of business" means a person that buys goods in good faith, without knowledge that the sale violates the rights of another person in the goods, and in the ordinary course from a person, other than a pawnbroker, in the business of selling goods of that kind. A person buys goods in the ordinary course if the sale to the person comports with the usual or customary practices in the kind of business in which the seller is engaged or with the seller's own usual or customary practices. A person that sells oil, gas, or other minerals at the wellhead or minehead is a person in the business of selling goods of that kind. A buyer in ordinary course of business may buy for cash, by exchange of other property, or on secured or unsecured credit, and may acquire goods or documents of

title under a preexisting contract for sale. Only a buyer that takes possession of the goods or has a right to recover the goods from the seller under Article 2 may be a buyer in ordinary course of business. "Buyer in ordinary course of business" does not include a person that acquires goods in a transfer in bulk or as security for or in total or partial satisfaction of a money debt.

(10) "Conspicuous", with reference to a term, means so written, displayed, or presented that a reasonable person against which it is to operate ought to have noticed it. Whether a term is "conspicuous" or not is a decision for the court. Conspicuous terms include the following:

(A) a heading in capitals equal to or greater in size than the surrounding text, or in contrasting type, font, or color to the surrounding text of the same or lesser size; and

(B) language in the body of a record or display in larger type than the surrounding text, or in contrasting type, font, or color to the surrounding text of the same size, or set off from surrounding text of the same size by symbols or other marks that call attention to the language.

(11) "Consumer" means an individual who enters into a transaction primarily for personal, family, or household purposes.

(12) "Contract", as distinguished from "agreement", means the total legal obligation that results from the parties' agreement as determined by [the Uniform Commercial Code] as supplemented by any other applicable laws.

(13) "Creditor" includes a general creditor, a secured creditor, a lien creditor, and any representative of creditors, including an assignee for the benefit of creditors, a trustee in bankruptcy, a receiver in equity, and an executor or administrator of an insolvent debtor's or assignor's estate.

(14) "Defendant" includes a person in the position of defendant in a counterclaim, cross-claim, or third-party claim.

(15) "Delivery", with respect to an electronic document of title means voluntary transfer of control and with respect to an instrument, a tangible document of title, or chattel paper, means voluntary transfer of possession.

(16) "Document of title" means a record (i) that in the regular course of business or financing is treated as adequately evidencing that the person in possession or control of the record is entitled to receive, control, hold, and dispose of the record and the goods the record covers and (ii) that purports to be issued by or addressed to a bailee and to cover goods in the bailee's possession which are either identified or are fungible portions of an identified mass. The term includes a bill of lading, transport document, dock warrant, dock receipt, warehouse receipt, and order for delivery of goods. An electronic document of title means a document of title evidenced by a record consisting of information stored in an electronic medium. A tangible document of title means a document of title evidenced by a record consisting of information that is inscribed on a tangible medium.

(17) "Fault" means a default, breach, or wrongful act or omission.

(18) "Fungible goods" means:
(A) goods of which any unit, by nature or usage of trade, is the equivalent of any other like unit; or

(B) goods that by agreement are treated as equivalent.

(19) "Genuine" means free of forgery or counterfeiting.

(20) "Good faith," except as otherwise provided in Article 5, means honesty in fact and the observance of reasonable commercial standards of fair dealing.

(21) "Holder" means:

 (A) the person in possession of a negotiable instrument that is payable either to bearer or to an identified person that is the person in possession;

 (B) the person in possession of a negotiable tangible document of title if the goods are deliverable either to bearer or to the order of the person in possession; or

 (C) the person in control of a negotiable electronic document of title.

(22) "Insolvency proceeding" includes an assignment for the benefit of creditors or other proceeding intended to liquidate or rehabilitate the estate of the person involved.

(23) "Insolvent" means:

 (A) having generally ceased to pay debts in the ordinary course of business other than as a result of bona fide dispute;

 (B) being unable to pay debts as they become due; or

 (C) being insolvent within the meaning of federal bankruptcy law.

(24) "Money" means a medium of exchange currently authorized or adopted by a domestic or foreign government. The term includes a monetary unit of account established by an intergovernmental organization or by agreement between two or more countries.

(25) "Organization" means a person other than an individual.

(26) "Party", as distinguished from "third-party", means a person that has engaged in a transaction or made an agreement subject to [the Uniform Commercial Code].

(27) "Person" means an individual, corporation, business trust, estate, trust, partnership, limited liability company, association, joint venture, government, governmental subdivision, agency, or instrumentality, public corporation, or any other legal or commercial entity.

(28) "Present value" means the amount as of a date certain of one or more sums payable in the future, discounted to the date certain by use of either an interest rate specified by the parties if that rate is not manifestly unreasonable at the time the transaction is entered into or, if an interest rate is not so specified, a commercially reasonable rate that takes into account the facts and circumstances at the time the transaction is entered into.

(29) "Purchase" means taking by sale, lease, discount, negotiation, mortgage, pledge, lien, security interest, issue or reissue, gift, or any other voluntary transaction creating an interest in property.

(30) "Purchaser" means a person that takes by purchase.

(31) "Record" means information that is inscribed on a tangible medium or that is stored in an electronic or other medium and is retrievable in perceivable form.

(32) "Remedy" means any remedial right to which an aggrieved party is entitled with or without resort to a tribunal.

(33) "Representative" means a person empowered to act for another, including an agent, an officer of a corporation or association, and a trustee, executor, or administrator of an estate.

(34) "Right" includes remedy.

(35) "Security interest" means an interest in personal property or fixtures which secures payment or performance of an obligation. "Security interest" includes any interest of a consignor and a buyer of accounts, chattel paper, a payment intangible, or a promissory note in a transaction that is subject to Article 9. "Security interest" does not include the special property interest of a buyer of goods on identification of those goods to a contract for sale under Section 2-401, but a buyer may also acquire a "security interest" by complying with Article 9. Except as otherwise provided in Section 2-505, the right of a seller or lessor of

goods under Article 2 or 2A to retain or acquire possession of the goods is not a "security interest", but a seller or lessor may also acquire a "security interest" by complying with Article 9. The retention or reservation of title by a seller of goods notwithstanding shipment or delivery to the buyer under Section 2-401 is limited in effect to a reservation of a "security interest." Whether a transaction in the form of a lease creates a "security interest" is determined pursuant to Section 1-203.

(36) "Send" in connection with a writing, record, or notice means:

    (A) to deposit in the mail or deliver for transmission by any other usual means of communication with postage or cost of transmission provided for and properly addressed and, in the case of an instrument, to an address specified thereon or otherwise agreed, or if there be none to any address reasonable under the circumstances; or

    (B) in any other way to cause to be received any record or notice within the time it would have arrived if properly sent.

(37) "Signed" includes using any symbol executed or adopted with present intention to adopt or accept a writing.

(38) "State" means a State of the United States, the District of Columbia, Puerto Rico, the United States Virgin Islands, or any territory or insular possession subject to the jurisdiction of the United States.

(39) "Surety" includes a guarantor or other secondary obligor.

(40) "Term" means a portion of an agreement that relates to a particular matter.

(41) "Unauthorized signature" means a signature made without actual, implied, or apparent authority. The term includes a forgery.

(42) "Warehouse receipt" means a document of title issued by a person engaged in the business of storing goods for hire.

(43) "Writing" includes printing, typewriting, or any other intentional reduction to tangible form. "Written" has a corresponding meaning.

§ 1-202. Notice; Knowledge.

(a) Subject to subsection (f), a person has "notice" of a fact if the person:

(1) has actual knowledge of it;

(2) has received a notice or notification of it; or

(3) from all the facts and circumstances known to the person at the time in question, has reason to know that it exists.

(b) "Knowledge" means actual knowledge. "Knows" has a corresponding meaning.

(c) "Discover", "learn", or words of similar import refer to knowledge rather than to reason to know.

(d) A person "notifies" or "gives" a notice or notification to another person by taking such steps as may be reasonably required to inform the other person in ordinary course, whether or not the other person actually comes to know of it.

(e) Subject to subsection (f), a person "receives" a notice or notification when:

(1) it comes to that person's attention; or

(2) it is duly delivered in a form reasonable under the circumstances at the place of business through which the contract was made or at another location held out by that person as the place for receipt of such communications.

(f) Notice, knowledge, or a notice or notification received by an organization is effective for a particular transaction from the time it is brought to the attention of the individual conducting that transaction and, in any event, from the time it would have been brought to the individual's attention if the organization had exercised due diligence. An organization exercises due diligence if it maintains reasonable routines for communicating significant information to the person conducting the transaction and there is reasonable compliance with the routines. Due diligence does not require an individual acting for the organization to communicate information unless the communication is part of the individual's regular duties or the individual has reason to know of the transaction and that the transaction would be materially affected by the information.

§ 1-203. Lease Distinguished From Security Interest.

(a) Whether a transaction in the form of a lease creates a lease or security interest is determined by the facts of each case.

(b) A transaction in the form of a lease creates a security interest if the consideration that the lessee is to pay the lessor for the right to possession and use of the goods is an obligation for the term of the lease and is not subject to termination by the lessee, and:

(1) the original term of the lease is equal to or greater than the remaining economic life of the goods;

(2) the lessee is bound to renew the lease for the remaining economic life of the goods or is bound to become the owner of the goods;

(3) the lessee has an option to renew the lease for the remaining economic life of the goods for no additional consideration or for nominal additional consideration upon compliance with the lease agreement; or

(4) the lessee has an option to become the owner of the goods for no additional consideration or for nominal additional consideration upon compliance with the lease agreement.

(c)   A transaction in the form of a lease does not create a security interest merely because:

   (1)   the present value of the consideration the lessee is obligated to pay the lessor for the right to possession and use of the goods is substantially equal to or is greater than the fair market value of the goods at the time the lease is entered into;

   (2)   the lessee assumes risk of loss of the goods;

   (3)   the lessee agrees to pay, with respect to the goods, taxes, insurance, filing, recording, or registration fees, or service or maintenance costs;

   (4)   the lessee has an option to renew the lease or to become the owner of the goods;

   (5)   the lessee has an option to renew the lease for a fixed rent that is equal to or greater than the reasonably predictable fair market rent for the use of the goods for the term of the renewal at the time the option is to be performed; or

   (6)   the lessee has an option to become the owner of the goods for a fixed price that is equal to or greater than the reasonably predictable fair market value of the goods at the time the option is to be performed.

(d)   Additional consideration is nominal if it is less than the lessee's reasonably predictable cost of performing under the lease agreement if the option is not exercised. Additional consideration is not nominal if:

   (1)   when the option to renew the lease is granted to the lessee, the rent is stated to be the fair market rent for the use of the goods for the term of the renewal determined at the time the option is to be performed; or

   (2)   when the option to become the owner of the goods is granted to the lessee, the price is stated to be the fair market value of the goods determined at the time the option is to be performed.

(e) The "remaining economic life of the goods" and "reasonably predictable" fair market rent, fair market value, or cost of performing under the lease agreement must be determined with reference to the facts and circumstances at the time the transaction is entered into.

§ 1-204. Value.

Except as otherwise provided in Articles 3, 4, [and] 5, [and 6], a person gives value for rights if the person acquires them:

(1) in return for a binding commitment to extend credit or for the extension of immediately available credit, whether or not drawn upon and whether or not a charge-back is provided for in the event of difficulties in collection;

(2) as security for, or in total or partial satisfaction of, a preexisting claim;

(3) by accepting delivery under a preexisting contract for purchase; or

(4) in return for any consideration sufficient to support a simple contract.

A. In General

Section 1-201(b) contains forty-three definitions of terms employed throughout the Code. A few, such as "consumer" in § 1-201(b)(11) and "record" in § 1-201(b)(31), are new. Several, such as "present value" in § 1-201(b)(28) have been borrowed from other articles (*see* § 2A-103(1)(u)). Others, like "buyer in ordinary course of business" in § 1-201(b)(9) have been amended because of changes in other articles or updated. Several definitions included in former § 1-201 that were long and complex have been segregated in whole or in part into separate sections, e.g., Notice and Knowledge (former § 1-201(25), (26), and (27)) in § 1-202; Lease Distinguished from Security Interest (formerly part of § 1-201(37)) in § 1-203; and Value (former § 1-201(44)) in § 1-204.

In addition, as previously noted in Chapter 2, each article of the Code has further definitions particular to that article and may also employ a few definitions from other articles. See, e.g., §§ 2-103 through 2-106. With certain exceptions, such as the definition of "good faith" in § 1-201(b)(20), which is discussed in Chapter 17, the definitions in Article 1 and other articles are not discussed in this primer; rather, they are discussed in the context of the substantive provisions in which they are employed.

Parties drafting a document should note that a court will not necessarily use the Code definition of a term in every context. Use of a Code definition for a non-Code purpose may or may not be sensible in a given case. For example, the term "bill of lading" is defined in § 1-201(b)(6). However, when a letter of credit used the term "full set clean on board bills of lading," the court in *Board of Trade of San Francisco v. Swiss Credit Bank*, 579 F.2d 146, 25 U.C.C. Rep. Serv. 1132 (9th Cir. 1979) (applying California law), stated that the definitions in the Code were for terms used in the Code and did not serve as a dictionary to be used in determining the meaning of terms in other contexts.

Additionally, use of a Code definition even for a Code purpose may not be sensible in a given case. For that reason, § 1-201(a) provides that "[u]nless the context otherwise requires," words or phrases defined in § 1-201(b), or in the additional definitions contained in other articles of the Code, have the meanings stated. Drafters on occasion insert in their contract a provision that states:

> Whenever a term defined by the Uniform Commercial Code is used in this agreement, the definition contained in the Code is to control.

Such a provision could be dangerous, as parties who are not thoroughly familiar with the Code definitions may not intend them to govern their agreement.

B. Undefined Terms

If the Code does not define a term, then a court is likely to use the ordinary, generally understood, meaning of the term. See *In re Golden Kernel, Inc.*, 5 U.C.C. Rep. Serv. 43 (E.D. Pa., Ref. 1968) (discussing the term "place of business"). A court, in employing a term, must be guided by the Code's purposes. See *In re Automated Bookbinding Services, Inc.*, 471 F.2d 546, 11 U.C.C. Rep. Serv. 897 (4th Cir. 1972) (applying Maryland law) (in defining "possession," the court must be guided by the Code's general purpose to create a precise guide for commercial transactions). It also is reasonable for a court to look to a defined term that is similar in wording or purpose to the undefined term. *Nat'l City Bank, Norwalk v. Golden Acre Turkeys, Inc.*, 65 Ohio St. 3d 371, 604 N.E.2d 149, 19 U.C.C. Rep. Serv. 2d 1213 (1992) (in determining the meaning of "farming operations," under former Article 9, the court looked to "farm products," which was a defined term).

A court also may look to other state law, particularly a statute and rule construction act of general applicability, for a definition. See *In re Atlantic Computer Systems, Inc.*, 135 B.R. 463, 16 U.C.C. Rep. Serv. 2d 1204 (Bankr. S.D. N.Y. 1992) (applying New York law) (for the definition of "bailee," the court must look to other state law), and *PYA/Monarch, Inc. v. Horner*, 72 Ohio App. 3d 791, 596 N.E.2d 515, 18 U.C.C. Rep. Serv. 2d 541 (1991) (in interpreting the word "concealed" as used in § 6-111, the court will apply a state statute on statute and rule construction stating that words that have acquired a technical or particular meaning shall be construed accordingly; thus, "concealed" should be given its "fixed legal signification").

CHAPTER

12

REASONABLE TIME AND SEASONABLENESS § 1-205

---

§ 1-205. Reasonable Time; Seasonableness.

(a) Whether a time for taking an action required by [the Uniform Commercial Code] is reasonable depends on the nature, purpose, and circumstances of the action.

(b) An action is taken seasonably if it is taken at or within the time agreed or, if no time is agreed, at or within a reasonable time.

A. Introduction

Many provisions in the Code require that a party act within a time period that is not specifically set, but rather is described as a "reasonable time." See, e.g., §§ 2A-516(3)(a) and 2-607(3)(a). As further described in Chapter 15, these are default rules, and under § 1-302(b), the parties may by agreement set a specific time or time period, but that period may not be "manifestly unreasonable." A prudent draftsperson makes liberal use of this right but takes care not to abuse it. This section provides some guidance to help determine 1) the measure of a reasonable time established by the Code when the parties do not establish a time period, and 2) whether a time period established by the parties is manifestly unreasonable.

B. Question of Fact

Reasonableness as to time is usually a question of fact. *Cardwell v. Int'l Housing, Inc.*, 282 Pa. Super. 498, 423 A.2d 355, 31 U.C.C. Rep. Serv. 512 (1980). Reasonableness as to time depends upon the nature, purpose, and circumstances of the action to be taken. See, e.g., *Tipton v. Woodbury,* 616 F.2d 170, 28 U.C.C. Rep. Serv. 1473 (5th Cir. 1980) (applying Florida law) (where buyer of securities sent a letter setting out the agreement to the seller almost three months after the oral agreement, the court found it nonetheless was sent within a reasonable time). A party must be prepared to provide evidence to show what constitutes a reasonable time. See, e.g., *In re Hardwick & Magee Co.*, 11 U.C.C. Rep. Serv. 1172 (D.C.E.D. Pa., Ref., 1972) (when seller, defending against a claim its retention of possession was fraudulent, introduced no evidence that its retention of the goods was for a commercially reasonable time, the court held against seller).

C. Manifestly Unreasonable

It may be difficult to violate § 1-302(b) by agreeing to a time period that is manifestly unreasonable, but it can be done. See, e.g., *Q. Vandenberg & Sons v. Siter,* 204 Pa. Super. 392, 204 A.2d 494, 2 U.C.C. Rep. Serv. 383 (Pa. 1964) (seller provided that all claims for defective merchandise had to be presented within eight days; court held while § 2-607(3)(a) requires notice of breach within a reasonable time and [§ 1-302(b)] allowed the parties to fix a time by agreement, a limitation that renders the warranties ineffective because latent defects are not reasonably discoverable within the limitation period is manifestly unreasonable). See also *General*

Electric Capital Corp. v. Nat'l Tractor Trailer School, Inc., 667 N.Y.S.2d 614, 175 Misc. 2d 20, 36 U.C.C. Rep. Serv. 2d 749 (requiring buyer to accept goods on delivery is manifestly unreasonable because it allows no time for inspection) and *Bead Chain Mfg. Co. v. Saxton Products, Inc.*, 183 Conn. 266, 439 A.2d 314, 31 U.C.C. Rep. Serv. 91 (1981) (striking down a "time is of the essence" clause under the circumstances present in that case).

D. Seasonable Time

On a few occasions, the Code requires that an action be taken "seasonably." See, e.g., §§ 2-207(1), 2-325(2), 2-607(5), and 3-119. Section 1-205(b) provides:

> An action is taken seasonably if it is taken at or
> within the time agreed or, if no time is agreed, at
> or within a reasonable time.

This provision then becomes circular, for to determine whether the action has been taken within a reasonable time, the test of subsection (1) would be used. Official Comment 2 contains the helpful reminder that the circumstances used in determining whether the parties have agreed to a particular time include course of dealing, course of performance, and usage of trade. Thus, where the parties have previously performed, the time they took to act will be relevant, and where they have not previously performed, the time parties in the trade take to act will be relevant.

CHAPTER

13

PRESUMPTIONS
§ 1-206

§ 1-206. Presumptions.

Whenever [the Uniform Commercial Code] creates a "presumption" with respect to a fact, or provides that a fact is "presumed," the trier of fact must find the existence of the fact unless and until evidence is introduced that supports a finding of its nonexistence.

This rule does not seem worthy of an entire provision. In fact, there is only one presumption in Article 2 (see § 2-513(4)) and none in Article 9. Its significance as a provision is that it does not really belong with the definitions, where it was found in former § 1-201(31), for rather than merely define a term, it commands the courts to do something, namely find the existence of a fact. Nevertheless, a handful of jurisdictions have left the provision in the definitions.

A good example of the workings of the rule is found in § 3-308(a). That subsection provides in part that "the signature

[on an instrument] is presumed to be authentic and authorized."
Official Comment 1 to that section provides in part:

> "Presumed" … means that until some evidence
> is introduced which would support a finding
> that the signature is forged or unauthorized, the
> plaintiff is not required to prove that it is valid. The
> presumption rests upon the fact that in ordinary
> experience forged or unauthorized signatures are
> very uncommon, and normally any evidence is
> within the control of, or more accessible to, the
> defendant. The defendant is therefore required
> to make some sufficient showing of the grounds
> for the denial before the plaintiff is required to
> introduce evidence.

CHAPTER

14

CHOICE OF LAW
§ 1-301

---

§ 1-301. Territorial Applicability; Parties' Power to Choose Applicable Law.

(a)   Except as otherwise provided in this section, when a transaction bears a reasonable relation to this state and also to another state or nation the parties may agree that the law either of this state or of such other state or nation shall govern their rights and duties.

(b)   In the absence of an agreement effective under subsection (a), and except as provided in subsection (c), [the Uniform Commercial Code] applies to transactions bearing an appropriate relation to this state.

(c)   If one of the following provisions of [the Uniform Commercial Code] specifies the applicable law, that provision governs and a contrary agreement is effective only to the extent permitted by the law so specified:

(1) Section 2-402;

(2) Sections 2A-105 and 2A-106;

(3) Section 4-102;

(4) Section 4A-507;

(5) Section 5-116;

[(6) Section 6-103;]

(7) Section 8-110;

(8) Sections 9-301 through 9-307.

A. Introduction

The fate of Revised § 1-301 provides some interesting insights into the uniform law process. The revisers made some substantial changes to former § 1-105(1), most importantly providing that parties were free to choose the law of a jurisdiction that did not bear a relation to the transaction. The revisers also created rules that applied when one of the parties was a consumer. These rules, consistent with the greater consumer protection built into more recent Code revisions, provided that the chosen law must bear a reasonable relation to the transaction, and could not deprive the consumer of protections granted by his or her state of residence.

The initial states that enacted Revised Article 1 did not enact these changes and instead enacted a rule similar to the former rule. The ULC ultimately withdrew the revised version, and replaced it with a version that made only stylistic changes to the former law. Thus, prior cases generally will remain good law. In many cases, of course, choice of law will not be significant because of the uniformity of Code provisions among jurisdictions. See, e.g., *Hatzlachh Supply Inc. v. Moishe's Electronics, Inc.*, 828 F. Supp. 178, 22 U.C.C. Rep. Serv. 2d 667 (S.D.N.Y. 1993) (because Code applicable to case was similar in New York and Texas—the two interested jurisdictions—no choice of law was required).

B. The Parties' Freedom to Choose the Governing Law

Section 1-301(a) permits the parties to choose the governing law as long as the transaction "bears a reasonable relation" to the chosen jurisdiction. It does not have to be the jurisdiction with the most significant contacts. In *Woods-Tucker Leasing Corp. of Georgia v. Hutcheson-Ingram Development Co.*, 642 F.2d 744, 30 U.C.C. Rep. Serv. 1505 (5th Cir. 1981) (applying Michigan law), the court upheld the choice of law agreement even though the state whose law was chosen had far fewer substantial contacts than the state whose law was not chosen. The court indicated that party autonomy should be limited only to the extent the parties select the law of a jurisdiction that has no normal relation to the transaction. Where two jurisdictions each had a relation to the transaction, the agreement of the parties selecting the law of one would be upheld. See also *Ward Transformer Co., Inc. v. Distrigas of Massachusetts Corp.*, 779 F. Supp. 823, 15 U.C.C. Rep. Serv. 2d 839 (E.D.N.C. 1991), and *In re Kemper*, 263 B.R. 773, 45 U.C.C. Rep. Serv. 2d 64 (Bankr. E.D. Tx. 2001).

Many jurisdictions also apply the rule found in Restatement (Second) of Conflict of Laws § 187 that the chosen law must not violate the policy of the jurisdiction whose law would have applied but for the choice of law provision. See, e.g., *El Pollo Loco, S.A. de C.V. v. El Pollo Loco, Inc.*, 344 F. Supp. 2d 986 (S.D. Tex. 2004). This issue is unlikely to arise unless one of the jurisdictions has enacted a nonuniform version of the Code provision in issue. In *Superfos Investments Ltd. v. First-Miss. Fertilizer, Inc.*, 809 F. Supp. 450, 20 U.C.C. Rep. Serv. 2d 4 (S.D. Miss. 1992), the parties chose Virginia law and pursuant to the Virginia enactment of § 2-725(1), reduced the four-year statute of limitations period to one year. Mississippi, however, had enacted a nonuniform version of § 2-725(1) that provided for a six-year statute instead of a four-year statute and did not permit the parties to reduce the duration.

The court nevertheless upheld the parties' choice of law, finding that it did not violate a fundamental public policy:

> The policy behind the Mississippi statute at issue, however, the purpose of which is to prevent contractual limitation of a statutory limitations period, cannot logically be viewed as being more fundamental a public policy of this state than the statutory limitations period itself. That is, since the Mississippi courts do not consider other state's substantive statutes of limitations so repugnant to Mississippi public policy that they would refuse to apply them, it cannot be reasonably concluded that another state's substantive statute which permits a contractual reduction of a statutory limitations period would be so offensive. Therefore, the court concludes that the Mississippi courts would give effect to the parties' choice of Virginia substantive law, including the limitations period included in the parties' agreement, with the result that the limitations provided by the parties contract—a valid provision under Virginia law—will be given effect where applicable.

There still are limits on choice of law agreements. First, it must be demonstrated that the provision was indeed agreed upon. See *Glyptal Inc. v. Engelhard Corp.*, 801 F. Supp. 887, 18 U.C.C. Rep. Serv. 2d 1059 (D. Mass. 1992) (court declined to take into account a choice of law provision in the seller's order acknowledgment form since a primary issue was whether the acknowledgment's terms were part of the parties' agreement). Second, the freedom of contracting parties to choose the applicable law when third parties may be affected also is limited as provided in § 1-301(c). Compare *Hong Kong & Shanghai Banking Corp., Ltd. v. HFH USA Corp.*, 805 F. Supp. 133, 19 U.C.C. Rep. Serv. 2d 885 (W.D.N.Y. 1992) (court refused to apply designated German law where the choice of law provision would work to the detriment of a third-party who was a stranger to the agreement), with *Diesel Props S.R.L. v. Greystone Business Credit II LLC*, 2008 WL 594773, 65 U.C.C. Rep. Serv. 2d 235 (S.D.N.Y. 2008) (enforcing provision stipulating Italian law and refusing to apply *Hong Kong & Shanghai Banking Corp., Ltd.* where sophisticated third party knew of and presumably understood the arrangement). Finally, party autonomy to choose applicable law may be limited by other law, such as a consumer protection statute. See, e.g., 1974 Uniform Consumer Credit Code § 1-201(4) and (8).

C. Choice of Law in the Absence of an Agreement

In the absence of an effective agreement choosing applicable law, § 1-301(b) provides that the Code, as enacted in a jurisdiction, may be applied to a transaction in accordance with the law of that jurisdiction as it would be selected by application of its conflict of laws principles. Those principles are not specified in relation to this provision. Under former § 1-105(1), a number of jurisdictions interpreted this as meaning the "most significant relation" test should be applied. See *In re Nantahala Village, Inc.*, 976 F.2d 876, 18 U.C.C. Rep. Serv. 2d 1027 (4th Cir. 1992) (applying Florida law) ("appropriate relation" should be interpreted to mean most significant relation); *Myrtle Beach Pipeline Corp. v. Emerson Elec. Co.*, 843 F. Supp. 1027, 23 U.C.C. Rep. Serv. 2d 683 (D.S.C. 1993) (the phrase "appropriate relation" has been construed as mirroring the "most significant relationship" test, but South Carolina would apply its law when it has a sufficiently "significant interest"); and *In re Merritt Dredging Co., Inc.*, 839 F.2d 203, 5 U.C.C. Rep. Serv. 2d 900 (4th Cir. 1988) (applying SC law) (the "most significant relationship" test used by a majority of courts best promotes the UCC policy of uniformity and predictability).

Whether the most significant relation test or some other approach is appropriate is left to the law of each jurisdiction. Official Comment 7 to the withdrawn version of this provision suggested that the provision "simply directs the forum to apply its ordinary choice of law principles to determine which jurisdiction's law governs." According to Restatement (Second) of Conflict of Laws § 6(2), relevant factors include:

(a)   the needs of the interstate and international systems,

(b)   the relevant policies of the forum,

(c)   the relevant policies of other interested states and the relative interests of those states in the determination of the particular issue,

(d)   the protection of justified expectations,

(e)   the basic policies underlying the particular field of law,

(f)   certainty, predictability and uniformity of result, and

(g)   ease in the determination and application of the law to be applied.

The purposes and policies of the Code found in § 1-103(a) should play a role in this context. See *In re Merritt Dredging Co., Inc.*, 839 F.2d 203, 5 U.C.C. Rep. Serv. 2d 900 (4th Cir. 1988) and *Butler v. Ford Motor. Co.*, 724 F. Supp. 2d 575, 72 U.C.C. Rep. Serv. 2d 691 (D.S.C. 2010) ("most significant relationship" test applied as best promoting the UCC policies of uniformity and predictability), and *In re High-Line Aviation, Inc.*, 149 B.R. 730, 20 U.C.C. Rep. Serv. 2d 12 (Bankr. N.D. Ga. 1992) (court should choose law that promotes rather than frustrates applicable UCC policy). In applying some of the above factors, Restatement (Second) of Conflict of Laws § 188 suggests that the following more particular matters should be considered in a case involving a contract:

(a)   the place of contracting,

(b)   the place of negotiation of the contract,

(c)   the place of performance,

(d)   the location of the subject matter of the contract, and

(e)   the domicil, residence, nationality, place of incorporation and place of business of the parties.

These contacts are to be evaluated according to their relative importance with respect to the particular issue.

D. The Exceptions—Where the Parties are not Free to Choose the Governing Law

The exceptions enumerated in § 1-301(c) to the general Code rule on choice of law reflect that some specific Code rules contained in other articles are not subject to variation by agreement, often because of the effect on third parties. These specific Code rules are as follows:

- the rule on which jurisdiction's law governs the rights of creditors against sold goods (§ 2-402);
- the applicability of Article 2A on leases with respect to certificate of title and consumer issues (§§ 2A-105 and 2A-106);
- the rule on bank liability in the choice of law rules in Article 4 on bank deposits and collections (§ 4-102);
- the choice of law rules in Article 4A on funds transfers (§ 4A-507);
- the choice of law rules in Article 5 on letters of credit (§ 5-116);
- the choice of law rules in Article 6 on bulk sales (§ 6-103);
- the choice of law rules in Article 8 on investment securities (§ 8-110); and
- the laws governing perfection and effect of perfection or nonperfection and the priority of a security interest (§§ 9-301 through 9-307).

Subsection (c)(6), referring to § 6-103, appears in brackets in the uniform version of the Code because a jurisdiction that has repealed Article 6 (Bulk Sales) does not enact it. The specific provisions are sometimes limited in scope. Thus, the restriction on choice of law when applied to § 9-301(3)(A) and (B), which is included in subsection (c)(8), extends no further than to govern the perfection of certain security interests. That is, the parties to a security agreement are free to choose the law of a jurisdiction that bears a reasonable relation to the transaction; however, that law will not apply to all issues. For example, in *Nat'l Pawn Brokers Unlimited v. Osterman, Inc.*, 176 Wis. 2d 418, 500 N.W.2d 407, 21 U.C.C. Rep. Serv. 2d 1176 (1993), where the parties chose Wisconsin law, the court held that Minnesota law governed whether an asserted security interest was perfected, but Wisconsin law governed whether the debtor had rights in the collateral so that the debtor could create an enforceable security interest. It also should be noted that the choice of law provisions in §§ 4A-507, 5-116, and 8-110 themselves allow variation by agreement—even to the extent of validating the parties' choice of law clause governing rights and obligations between each other when it bears no reasonable relation to the jurisdiction whose law is chosen.

When dealing with a multistate transaction, therefore, it is important to examine any agreement between the parties and to bear the exceptions in § 1-301(c) in mind. It also is important to remember that the exceptions to the power of the parties to choose the governing law by contract in certain circumstances may vary from state to state. The law of each state to which the transaction relates should be checked to make sure that the parties have adopted an enforceable choice of law provision.

E. International Transactions

Note that the provision has application in international transactions as well. Compare, e.g., *Callahan Equipment Co. v. Markarian*, 34 U.C.C. Rep. Serv. 1503 (D.N.J. 1982) (the fact that the place of delivery of goods was Iran did not outweigh substantial contacts with New Jersey, including forum state, situs of seller, place of contract negotiation, and place for payment), *with Windsor Indus., Inc. v. Eaca Int'l Ltd.*, 548 F. Supp. 635, 34 U.C.C. Rep. Serv. 1095 (E.D.N.Y. 1982) (negotiations for sale, buyer's orders received, delivery to agent, and payment by letters of credit established in Hong Kong dictated that law of Hong Kong would apply).

Increasingly, there are international treaties or conventions that may apply in transactions between persons in different countries. Assume a sale transaction in which the seller is located in Germany and the buyer in Virginia, the issue concerns performance of the contract, and delivery of the goods occurred in Germany. On these facts, the court in *Madaus v. November Hill Farm, Inc.*, 630 F. Supp. 1246, 1 U.C.C. Rep. Serv. 2d 24 (W.D. Va. 1986), held German law applicable. Since then, both the United States and Germany have adopted the United Nations Convention on Contracts for the International Sale of Goods (CISG). Were the case to arise today, under CISG Article 1(1), the CISG would apply to the contract because it involves commercial parties that have places of business in different states (i.e., countries), and both are contracting states (i.e., they have both adopted the CISG). A table showing which countries have adopted the CISG can be found at http://www.cisg. law.pace.edu/cisg/countries/cntries.html.

CISG Article 6 provides that the parties may choose law that "excludes the application of this Convention." Many U.S. attorneys take advantage of that option by inserting in their international agreements a choice of law clause in which the parties choose the UCC of their jurisdiction. In preparing the choice of law provision, keep in mind the notorious rule of *Asante Technologies, Inc. v. PMC-Sierra, Inc.*, 164 F. Supp. 2d 1142 (N.D. Cal. 2001). That case held that a choice of "California law" in a contract involving the international sales of goods was not sufficient to opt out of application of the CISG because the CISG *was* the law of California. The careful drafter should be more specific, providing for the "California UCC" to govern, and perhaps adding, "The parties specifically exclude application of the CISG."

CHAPTER

15

VARIATION BY AGREEMENT
§ 1-302

§ 1-302. Variation by Agreement.

(a) Except as otherwise provided in subsection (b) or elsewhere in [the Uniform Commercial Code], the effect of provisions of [the Uniform Commercial Code] may be varied by agreement.

(b) The obligations of good faith, diligence, reasonableness, and care prescribed by [the Uniform Commercial Code] may not be disclaimed by agreement. The parties, by agreement, may determine the standards by which the performance of those obligations is to be measured if those standards are not manifestly unreasonable. Whenever [the Uniform Commercial Code] requires an action to be taken within a reasonable time, a time that is not manifestly unreasonable may be fixed by agreement.

(c) The presence in certain provisions of [the Uniform Commercial Code] of the phrase "unless otherwise agreed", or words of similar import, does not imply that the effect of other provisions may not be varied by agreement under this section.

A. Freedom of Contract

Overall, the effect of most provisions of the Code can be varied by agreement. In this context, the Code is like a safety net. For the most part, it does not provide rules that must be followed, but rather rules that will govern absent a different resolution by agreement. In this sense, the Code is facilitatory rather than mandatory—it facilitates the making of transactions rather than regulating them. A lawyer must always determine whether to follow the Code default rule or vary it. For this reason, it is important to know what the default rule is and whether there are any restrictions on varying it.

Section 1-302 establishes a broad policy favoring freedom of contract in commercial dealings and flexibility through agreement, including custom and usage in accordance with § 1-303. See generally §§ 1-103(a)(2), 1-302(a), and 1-303. See also, e.g., *Colorado Interstate Gas Co., Inc. v. Chemco, Inc.*, 833 P.2d 786, 17 U.C.C. Rep. Serv. 2d 1162 (Colo. App. 1991), *aff'd* 854 P.2d 1232, 23 U.C.C. Rep. Serv. 2d 433 (Colo. 1993) (parties by agreement can vary the provisions of the UCC), and *Bausch & Lomb, Inc. v. Bressler,* 977 F.2d 720, 18 U.C.C. Rep. Serv. 2d 1130 (2d Cir. 1992) (applying New York law) (provisions of contract controlled over remedy provisions of Article 2). Various Code articles additionally contain their own explicit expression of the parties' freedom of contract. See, e.g., § 4-103(a) *and Scott Stainless Steel, Inc. v. NBD Chicago Bank,* 253 Ill. App. 3d 256, 625 N.E.2d 293, 24 U.C.C. Rep. Serv. 2d 609 (1993).

B. Limitations on Agreement

The first sentence of § 1-302(b) initially takes away that freedom with respect to "the obligations of good faith, diligence, reasonableness, and care." See, e.g., *Butler Mfg. Co. v. Ameri-cold Corp.*, 835 F. Supp. 1274, 22 U.C.C. Rep. Serv. 2d 318 (D. Kan. 1993) (warehouseman's attempt to disclaim liability for ordinary negligence and allow recovery only for gross negligence or willful injury not enforceable), and *Sybedon Corp. v. Bank Leumi Trust Co. of New York,* 22 U.C.C. Rep. Serv. 2d 1111 (N.Y. Sup. Ct. 1994) (bank cannot disclaim its duty of ordinary care). There also are specific limitations in various articles. See, e.g., §§ 4A-202(f) and 4-103(a) and *Gillen v. Maryland Nat'l Bank,* 274 Md. 96, 333 A.2d 329, 16 U.C.C. Rep. Serv. 1067 (Ct. App. 1975) (duty of bank to use ordinary care cannot be abrogated by agreement). See also §§ 4A-501 and 9-602. In some cases a specific formula must be followed to disclaim an obligation. See, e.g., §§ 2-316(2) and 2A-214(2).

Furthermore, some provisions may not be varied even though they do not explicitly say so; unconscionability in §§ 2-302 and 2A-108 are likely examples. Official Comment 1 states in part:

> This principle of freedom of contract is subject to specific exceptions found elsewhere in the Uniform Commercial Code and to the general exception stated here. The specific exceptions vary in explicitness: the statute of frauds found in Section 2-201, for example, does not explicitly preclude oral waiver of the requirement of a writing, but a fair reading denies enforcement to such a waiver as part of the "contract" made unenforceable; Section 9-602, on the other hand, is a quite explicit limitation on freedom of contract.

See, e.g., *Becker v. Nat'l Bank and Trust Co.,* 222 Va. 716, 284 S.E.2d 793, 32 U.C.C. Rep. Serv. 1083 (1981) (court determined that the parties by agreement could not change the meaning of certain defined terms or fundamental concepts, as noted in what is now Official Comment 1).

C. Parties' Determination of Standards

The second sentence of 1-302(b) restores some of that freedom, with an important restriction. The parties are allowed to "determine the standards by which the performance of those obligations is to be measured if those standards are not manifestly unreasonable."

The Code does not explain what makes a standard "manifestly unreasonable." The UCC methodology is to have the meaning of such vague terms determined contextually by either the trade or the courts. As far as the trade goes, Official Comment 1 points out that "[i]n this connection, Section 1-303 incorporating into the agreement prior course of dealing and usages of trade is of particular importance." Parties seeking to employ trade usage might incorporate the following language rom 4 U.L.A. 24 Form 2 (2007):

> **Clause Adopting Standards of Good Faith, Diligence, Reasonableness, and Care.** Unless expressly provided otherwise herein, compliance with or observance of the standards set forth in the [list of any applicable industrial, commercial, financial or other group whose customs, code of ethics or like standards are generally recognized and which are acceptable to the parties] shall constitute the observance of good faith, diligence, reasonableness and care with respect to the matters covered thereby.

Many of the decided cases in which the courts have examined whether the parties' agreed standards are enforceable come from Article 9. While § 9-602 contains a lengthy list of rights and duties that may not be waived or varied, § 9-603 contains a provision analogous to § 1-302, permitting the parties to agree to "standards measuring the fulfillment of the rights of a debtor or obligor and the duties of a secured party under a rule stated in Section 9-602 if the standards are not manifestly unreasonable." One important exception: § 9-603(b) expressly provides that the parties may not determine standards for what constitutes breach of the peace.

At one extreme are provisions that simply negate the UCC obligation. For example, if a security agreement provided that the creditor had the right on default to immediately retain the collateral, it would seem that a court could strike the provision as violating § 9-602 without even attempting to determine standards. But in *Morgan Buildings & Spas, Inc. v. Turn-Key Leasing, Ltd.*, 97 S.W.3d 871, 49 U.C.C. Rep. Serv. 2d 941 (Tex. App. 2003), the Texas Court of Appeals thought it should at least determine whether such a provision was manifestly unreasonable under the former UCC equivalent of § 9-603. For that purpose, it looked to the definition of *manifest* in *Black's Law Dictionary*, which is "evident to the senses, especially to the sight, obvious to the understanding, evident to the mind, not obscure or hidden, and is synonymous with open, clear, visible, unmistakable, indubitable, evident, and self-evident." Under that standard, the surrender of rights was found to be manifestly unreasonable.

Moving from the extreme, a more typical approach is found in *Orix Credit Alliance, Inc. v. East End Development Corp.*, 260 A.D.2d 454, 688 N.Y.S.2d 191, 39 U.C.C. Rep. Serv. 2d 596 (App. Div. 1999), where the security agreement contained "provisions concerning prior notice to the debtors of the public sale of the collateral, prior newspaper advertisement of the sale, and mandatory terms of purchase at a public sale." The New York Appellate Division first articulated the purpose of the former UCC equivalent of § 9-602 as "prohibiting agreements which relieve secured creditors from virtually all responsibility with respect to the collateral." It then determined that the agreed standards of commercial reasonableness did not effectively leave the creditor free of those duties. Therefore, they were not manifestly unreasonable. This is a sound approach, which recognizes that there are many reasonable ways to perform a particular task.

In *Leonia Bank PLC v. Kouri*, 286 A.D.2d 654, 730 N.Y.S.2d 501, 46 U.C.C. Rep. Serv. 2d 253 (App. Div. 2001), the parties after default agreed that the creditor had an option to purchase pledged artwork from a guarantor at certain prices. Even though the option was exercised more than two years later, the New York Appellate Division found that the agreement was not manifestly unreasonable, since "both debtor and creditor were protected against subsequent fluctuations in value."

In *Ford Motor Credit Co. v. Solway*, 825 F.2d 1213, 4 U.C.C. Rep. Serv. 2d 630 (7th Cir. 1987) (applying Illinois law), Ford foreclosed on the inventory of a dealership. The security agreement provided that a private sale in which Ford solicited bids from at least three dealers, and accepted the highest bid, was commercially reasonable. The Seventh Circuit upheld this standard, stating that "[w]here a security agreement deems a particular means of disposing of the collateral to be commercially reasonable, then compliance with that provision is strong evidence that the secured party's disposition of the collateral was commercially reasonable."

See also *Federal Deposit Insurance Corp. v. Caliendo*, 802 F. Supp. 575, 18 U.C.C. Rep. Serv. 2d 899 (D.N.H. 1992) (duty to exercise reasonable care may be contractually altered provided that the duty as defined is not manifestly unreasonable), and *Tennessee Gas Pipeline Co. v. Lenape Resources Corp.*, 870 S.W.2d 286, 24 U.C.C. Rep. Serv. 2d 45 (Tex. App. 1993), *reh'g denied* January 26, 1994 (parties may determine standards by which to measure the performance of good faith and reasonableness, but standard must be clear, specific, and not unreasonable).

It appears that, at least in Article 9, courts are quite tolerant of the parties' attempts to agree to standards that measure UCC obligations as long as the standards do not effectively negate the function of the UCC rule. If a creditor contemplates an action that may be questionable after the fact, it would be prudent to provide in the agreement that the parties agree that the standard is commercially reasonable.

As a practical matter, it is important that the parties follow the agreed-upon standards. In a number of the reported cases, the court did not have to analyze whether the standards were manifestly unreasonable because the parties neglected to adhere to the agreed-upon standards. This could be quite a setback for the creditor. For example, § 9-610(a) provides that a creditor must provide notification of disposition within a reasonable time; § 9-610(b) then provides that ten days' notice is a safe harbor. Assume the parties agree in advance to eight days' notice. If the creditor gave eight days' notice, then it would only have to prove that this standard was not manifestly unreasonable. But if the creditor failed to comply with its own agreement by giving seven days' notice, then it would not get the benefit of either the statutory safe harbor or the agreed-upon safe harbor.

D. Effect on Third Parties

The parties may not, through agreement among themselves, vary provisions intended for the protection of third parties, such as the rules in Article 9 relating to the perfection of security interests. See, e.g., *Prime Financial Services LLC v. Vinton*, 279 Mich. App. 245, 761 N.W.2d 694, 65 U.C.C. Rep. Serv. 2d 867 (2008). Official Comment 1 provides in part:

> The effect of an agreement on the rights of third parties is left to specific provisions of the Uniform Commercial Code and to supplementary principles applicable under Section 1-103. The rights of third parties under Section 9-317 when a security interest is unperfected, for example, cannot be destroyed by a clause in the security agreement.

But see §§ 4-103(b), 4A-501(b), and 8-111, and perhaps 5-116(c), where "system" rules or agreements may impact indirect participants. To illustrate, § 4-301 allows a bank two business days to decide whether or not to pay a check presented otherwise than for immediate payment over the counter that its customer has drawn on the customer's account. This means a check received on Friday must be paid or returned by the close of business on Monday. In the case of *West Side Bank v. Marine Nat'l Exchange Bank*, 37 Wis. 2d 661, 155 N.W.2d 587, 4 U.C.C. Rep. Serv. 1003 (1968), the check was returned on Tuesday. Nonetheless, the court held this was proper since the clearinghouse rules between the banks had varied the effect of § 4-301 by agreement as permitted in § 4-103(b). In effect, the court found that by participating in a system that had adopted its own rules, the parties had each "agreed" to those system rules and were bound to them.

E. Section 1-302(c)

Section 1-302(c) cleans up some careless drafting in the Code. Some provisions expressly state that they are subject to the parties' power to vary the provision. This subsection reminds us that the failure of any section to expressly state that the parties have the ability to vary it by agreement does not imply that freedom of contract is abrogated. However, as noted in Part B above, it does not necessarily mean that they *have* the power to vary it, as some provisions may state immutable rules.

CHAPTER
16

COURSE OF PERFORMANCE, COURSE OF DEALING, AND USAGE OF TRADE
§ 1-303

§ 1-303. Course of Performance, Course of Dealing, and Usage of Trade.

(a) A "course of performance" is a sequence of conduct between the parties to a particular transaction that exists if:

(1) the agreement of the parties with respect to the transaction involves repeated occasions for performance by a party; and

(2) the other party, with knowledge of the nature of the performance and opportunity for objection to it, accepts the performance or acquiesces in it without objection.

(b) A "course of dealing" is a sequence of conduct concerning previous transactions between the parties to a particular transaction that is fairly to be regarded as establishing a common basis of understanding for interpreting their expressions and other conduct.

(c)   A "usage of trade" is any practice or method of dealing having such regularity of observance in a place, vocation, or trade as to justify an expectation that it will be observed with respect to the transaction in question. The existence and scope of such a usage must be proved as facts. If it is established that such a usage is embodied in a trade code or similar record, the interpretation of the record is a question of law.

(d)   A course of performance or course of dealing between the parties or usage of trade in the vocation or trade in which they are engaged or of which they are or should be aware is relevant in ascertaining the meaning of the parties' agreement, may give particular meaning to specific terms of the agreement, and may supplement or qualify the terms of the agreement. A usage of trade applicable in the place in which part of the performance under the agreement is to occur may be so utilized as to that part of the performance.

(e)   Except as otherwise provided in subsection (f), the express terms of an agreement and any applicable course of performance, course of dealing, or usage of trade must be construed whenever reasonable as consistent with each other. If such a construction is unreasonable:
   (1)   express terms prevail over course of performance, course of dealing, and usage of trade;
   (2)   course of performance prevails over course of dealing and usage of trade; and
   (3)   course of dealing prevails over usage of trade.

(f)   Subject to Section 2-209 and Section 2A-208, a course of performance is relevant to show a waiver or modification of any term inconsistent with the course of performance.

(g)   Evidence of a relevant usage of trade offered by one party is not admissible unless that party has given the other party notice that the court finds sufficient to prevent unfair surprise to the other party.

A. Introduction

The parties to an agreement on a subject covered by the Code often have dealt with each other before, either in a past transaction or in the transaction at hand if it involves more than one performance. The first situation is known as course of dealing (see § 1-303(b)), and the latter is known as course of performance (see § 1-303(a)). Even if they have never dealt with each other, they may have in common usages of the trade of which they are a part (see § 1-303(c)). The parties to a transaction subject to the Code enter and perform a transaction against this background of trade usage, past dealings, or previous performances, all of which may give particular meaning to or supplement or qualify their agreement. § 1-303(d).

B. "Agreement" in the Code

"Agreement" has a broader meaning in Code transactions than just the record or oral bargain of the parties. Section 1-201(b)(3) defines "agreement" to include terms arising from not only the record or oral bargain of the parties, but also from course of dealing, usage of trade, or course of performance. The Code makes the practical presumption that parties conduct their transactions in accordance with the prevailing customs and practices of their place, vocation, or trade (usage of trade) and in the same manner as they have dealt with each other in previous transactions (course of dealing) or earlier in the same transaction (course of performance). See § 1-303(a), (b), and (c) and *Heggblade-Marguleas-Tenneco, Inc. v. Sunshine Biscuit, Inc.*, 131 Cal. Rptr. 183, 19 U.C.C. Rep. Serv. 1067 (Ct. App. 1976) (writings are to be read on assumption that usages of trade were taken for granted when document was phrased).

Usage of trade, course of dealing, and course of performance can be thought of as implied terms that may form part of an agreement in spite of the parties' failure to expressly include them. Recall that the Article 2 parol evidence rule, § 2-202(a), provides that usage of trade, course of dealing, and course of performance are permissible to explain or supplement even a fully integrated agreement; that is, they will be admissible in spite of the presence of a merger clause that excludes terms not found in the writing. See, e.g., *Stinnes Interoil, Inc. v. Apex Oil Co.*, 604 F. Supp. 978, 41 U.C.C. Rep. Serv. 1293 (S.D.N.Y. 1985) (applying Missouri law) (court held that a merger clause in a writing did not preclude the seller from proving that the parties, through usage of trade and their prior course of dealing and performance, intended the agreement to be an installment contract); *Dangerfield v. Markel*, 222 N.W.2d 373, 15 U.C.C. Rep. Serv. 765 (N.D. 1974) (court stated that evidence of a custom or usage in the trade may be used to explain ambiguous portions of an agreement); *Keck v. Wacker*, 413 F. Supp. 1377, 20 U.C.C. Rep. Serv. 94 (E.D. Ky. 1976) (applying Kentucky law) (custom was used to show the meaning of the terms "barren" and "slipped" in reference to a sale of a horse); *Atlan Indus., Inc. v. O.E.M., Inc.*, 555 F. Supp. 184, 35 U.C.C. Rep. Serv. 795 (W.D. Okla. 1983) (applying Oklahoma law) (industry practice was used to define the duties of the buyer under the contract when the agreement did not speak to the point); *Mechanics Nat'l Bank of Worcester v. Gaucher*, 386 N.E.2d 1052, 25 U.C.C. Rep. Serv. 1313 (Mass. Ct. App. 1979) (court stated that usage of trade may be tantamount to an "otherwise agreed" condition); and *In re Bailey Pontiac, Inc.*, 139 B.R. 629, 18 U.C.C. Rep. Serv. 2d 127 (N.D. Texas 1992) (applying both Montana and Texas law where both states had significant relationships with the transaction and applicable Code provisions were the same in both states) (custom and practice of the auction industry was held to control the question of when title to vehicles passed). For a case where the dissent argued that the result was erroneous because the majority had ignored a meaning established by the parties over a seventeen-year course of dealing, see *Octagon Gas Systems, Inc. v. Rimmer*, 995 F.2d 948, 20 U.C.C. Rep. Serv. 2d 1330 (10th Cir. 1993) (applying Oklahoma law), *cert, denied,* 510 U.S. 993 (1993).

In addition to consulting the statute, a lawyer should always consider the agreement of the parties and any trade usage or particular dealings of the parties that might bear on the issue. Cases indicating that course of dealing, course of performance, and usage of trade may be part of the agreement include *Capitol Converting Equip., Inc. v. Lep Transport, Inc.*, 750 F. Supp. 862, 14 U.C.C. Rep. Serv. 2d 51 (N.D. Ill. 1990) (applying Illinois law) (course of dealing is an integral part of a contract); *Vermilion County Production Credit Ass'n v. Izzard*, 111 Ill. App. 2d 190, 249 N.E.2d 352, 6 U.C.C. Rep. Serv. 940 (1969) (course of dealing or usage of trade are factors in determining the commercial meaning of the agreement); and *Brunswick Box Co., Inc. v. Coutinho, Caro & Co., Inc.*, 617 F.2d 355, 28 U.C.C. Rep. Serv. 616 (4th Cir. 1980) (applying Virginia law) (agreement is the bargain of the parties as found in their language, and any relevant course of dealing, usage of trade, or course of performance as being relevant in determining the meaning of the parties).

Specifically, a course of dealing or performance between the parties and any usage of trade are relevant in ascertaining the meaning of the agreement. They also may give particular meaning to specific terms and supplement or qualify the terms of an agreement. § 1-303(d). See, e.g., *Pennzoil Co. v. Federal Energy Regulatory Commission*, 645 F.2d 360, 31 U.C.C. Rep. Serv. 1242 (5th Cir. 1981) (applying Code as federal common law) (court held that evidence as to course of performance and usage of trade was properly considered in determining the intent of the parties to natural gas sale contracts as to whether "area rate clauses" in the contracts could escalate the contract price to the maximum lawful price). Similar holdings were made in *Loeb & Co., Inc. v. Martin*, 327 So. 2d 711, 18 U.C.C. Rep. Serv. 854 (Ala. 1976) (custom and usage was admissible to explain meaning of handwritten memorandum); *Jazel Corp. v. Sentinel Enterprises, Inc.*, 20 U.C.C. Rep. Serv. 837 (N.Y. Sup. Ct. 1976) (usage of trade was admissible to explain or supplement the written agreement); *Koenen v. Royal Buick Co.*, 162 Ariz. 376, 783 P.2d 822, 11 U.C.C. Rep. Serv. 2d 1096 (Ariz. App. 1989) (course of dealing could be used to supply missing price term when buyer had always paid sticker price in past); and *Central Washington Production Credit Ass'n v. Baker,* 11 Wash. App. 17, 521 P.2d 226, 14 U.C.C. Rep. Serv. 1055 (1974) (course of conduct may be used to show consent of secured party to sale of collateral).

Of course, the parties are free to contract around this rule. See § 1-302(a). They could, for example, include a provision stating:

> No course of prior dealings between the parties and
> no usage of trade shall be relevant to supplement
> or explain any term used in this agreement.

Such a provision must be used with caution, however. One reason course of dealing and usage of trade are implied in the agreement is that they unconsciously form part of the parties' expectations under the contract. If the parties are not fully conscious of the assumptions they have made, then they should not exclude them from the agreement.

C. Course of Performance

Prior to the revision of Article 1, the concept of course of performance was found in Articles 2 and 2A. It has now been combined in § 1-303 with the concepts of course of dealing and trade usage, thus making clear that the concept applies, like the other provisions of Article 1, throughout the Code. See § 1-102.

A course of performance arises when there are repeated occasions for performance by a party under the same contract. (If there are repeated occasions for performance by a party under prior contracts between the same parties, then a course of dealing may arise.) The course of performance arises only if the other party accepts the performance or acquiesces to it without objection. A party who does not wish to establish a course of performance must affirmatively object to the performance. It is unlikely that a single performance can constitute a course of performance; Official Comment 4 to § 2-208, which is repealed when a jurisdiction enacts § 1-303, provided in part that "[a] single occasion of conduct does not fall within the language of this section."

Course of performance might, for example, establish what the parties mean by a "reasonable" time after one party has performed on a number of occasions at a particular time. It can also lead to the waiver of a right. A typical case arose in *Nevada Nat'l Bank v. Huff*, 94 Nev. 506, 582 P.2d 364, 24 U.C.C. Rep. Serv. 1044 (1978) where a secured creditor repossessed a truck pursuant to a term in the contract permitting repossession on default. On the debtor's claim for wrongful repossession, the court stated:

> It was a common occurrence for Huff to be behind in his monthly payments. In fact, Huff had been late with every single payment under the truck lease. Further, he had been two payments behind on two occasions, and three payments behind on one occasion. In spite of these delinquencies, NNB had never declared a default or invoked its right to repossess.... Rather, written and oral demands for payment had always been made upon him, and payment had always quickly followed.

This course of conduct established between Huff and NNB imposed upon NNB the duty, before it could properly rely upon the default and repossession clauses in the lease agreement, to give notice to Huff that strict compliance with the terms of the long-ignored contract would henceforth be required in order to avert repossession of the vehicle. Upon NNB's failure to give such notice, the jury could properly have concluded that NNB's repossession of the truck was wrongful.

D. Course of Dealing

Section 1-303(b) defines "course of dealing" as actions in past transactions between the parties that are indicative of their future actions. Consider *Provident Tradesmen's Bank and Trust Co. v. Pemberton*, 173 A.2d 780, 1 U.C.C. Rep. Serv. 57 (Pa. 1961). In that case, an auto dealer sold an automobile, which was financed for the buyer by the plaintiff bank. A security interest in the car was given to the bank, and, as was the practice between them, the dealer guaranteed the buyer's obligation. As was customary, the bank required the buyer to insure the car. The car subsequently was wrecked. The insurance company paid to have it repaired but then cancelled the insurance. The bank did not notify the dealer of the cancellation, even though it had done so in past cases so that the dealer could take steps to obtain insurance to protect itself on the guaranty. The car was wrecked again. The buyer defaulted on the obligation, and since the car was now worth little and there was no insurance, the bank sued the dealer on the guaranty, claiming the difference between the reduced value of the car and the unpaid balance.

Even though the form agreement between the bank and the dealer provided that all notices whatsoever in respect to the security agreement were waived, the court held that under what is now § 1-303, the past course of dealing required that this clause be interpreted to mean only those notices mentioned in the text of the agreement were waived. The waiver did not include all notices given in the past by the bank to the dealer. Past course of dealing gave particular meaning to and supplemented the agreement, requiring the bank to give notice of the insurance cancellation.

E. Usage of Trade

The parties to a transaction also may be expected to contract against the background of any practice or method of dealing having regularity of observance in their location, or in their vocation or trade, and that "usage of trade" as defined in § 1-303(c) may also give particular meaning to, supplement, or qualify the agreement between them. § 1-303(d).

For example, issuers of letters of credit commonly incorporate in a letter of credit the Uniform Customs and Practice for Documentary Credits (UCP), currently published by the International Chamber of Commerce as I.C.C. Pub. No. 600. This document represents widely adhered to international practices also applicable in domestic situations. See e.g., *Banca del Sempione v. Suriel Finance, N.V.*, 852 F. Supp. 417, 24 U.C.C. Rep. Serv. 2d 1196 (D. Md. 1994) (applying Maryland law). Even if issuers of letters of credit do not incorporate the UCP, it often can be assumed that they contract against it as background. Indeed, § 5-103 Official Comment 2 states that it is appropriate for the parties and the courts to turn to customs and practice such as the UCP even if not specifically referred to, that is, if the letter of credit is silent. The UCP, or a similar group of practices or method of dealing, is an example of a usage of trade under § 1-303.

A usage of trade will be allowed to supplement the terms of the agreement when there is evidence that both parties knew or should have known of that usage. *Atlantic Track & Turnout Co. v. Perini Corp.*, 989 F.2d 541, 20 U.C.C. Rep. Serv. 2d 426 (1st Cir. 1993) (applying Massachusetts law). See also *Adams v. American Cyanamid Co.*, 498 N.W.2d 577, 21 U.C.C. Rep. Serv. 2d 962 (Neb. App. 1992), and *Martin Rispens & Son v. Hall Farms, Inc.*, 601 N.E.2d 429, 19 U.C.C. Rep. Serv. 2d 1021 (Ind. App. 1992) (holding that knowledge of trade usage is imputed to those who undertake business transactions in the industry, regardless of their level of experience therein).

Section 1-303(c) more fully defines "usage of trade" as what regularly is practiced by others in a similar place, vocation, or trade relevant to a transaction so that it is expected to be observed in the transaction in question. Consider *Posttapes Associates v. Eastman Kodak Co.*, 450 F. Supp. 407, 23 U.C.C. Rep. Serv. 855 (E.D. Pa. 1977) (applying Pennsylvania law). In that case, the plaintiff purchased some film for the production of a documentary motion picture. The film contained a latent defect which rendered the production worthless. In the plaintiff's suit, the defendant showed that a usage of trade of the commercial film industry was that a manufacturer's liability for faulty film was limited to replacement of the raw stock. This limit is due to the difficulty of discovering latent defects and the vast differences in uses of the film. This was an expensive lesson, but fortunately the plaintiff did not have to bear the full expense because he had purchased "raw stock" insurance against such latent defects (which the court also considered to be indicative of the prevalence and acceptance of the claimed trade usage). See § 1-303(c) and (d).

In another case, still relevant although pre-Code, the plaintiff was not so fortunate. In *L. Gillarde Co. v. Martinelli & Co.*, 168 F.2d 276 (1st Cir. 1948) (applying NY law), *reh'g granted*, 169 F.2d 60 (1st Cir. 1948), a seller sold a carload of cantaloupes, infected with a rot that made them unmerchantable, on a "rolling acceptance final" basis. The buyer refused to accept them when they arrived. Under the Code, the buyer would have this right to reject under § 2-601. However, the court held that in the trade the "rolling acceptance final" provision had a clear meaning: there was no right of rejection, only a right to damage recovery. On rehearing, the court further stated that under trade usage a wrongful rejection further deprived the buyer of any damage recourse whatsoever.

F. Limitations

There are limitations, however, on the use of course of dealing, course of performance, and usage of trade. First, they may be used to interpret an agreement but not to create obligations when no agreement exists. Thus, in the absence of any evidence of an agreement between a bank and payees of dishonored checks, concerning the payment of funds from a depositor's account, the bank's past practice of honoring checks on the account when it contained insufficient funds did not show the bank had an obligation to honor checks. *In re Smith*, 51 B.R. 904, 41 U.C.C. Rep. Serv. 804 (Bankr. M.D. Ga. 1985) (applying Georgia law). By the same token, trade usage can be used to fill in gaps in a contract, but it cannot create a new obligation. *Capitol Converting Equipment, Inc. v. Lep Transp., Inc.* 750 F. Supp. 862, 14 U.C.C. Rep. Serv. 2d 51 (N.D. Ill. 1990) (applying Illinois law).

Second, a course of performance or dealing or usage of trade may not be used to displace or negate established rules of law that cannot otherwise be changed by agreement. *Vermilion County Production Credit Ass'n v. Izzard,* 111 Ill. App. 2d 190, 249 N.E.2d 352, 6 U.C.C. Rep. Serv. 940 (1969).

Third, while the express terms of an agreement and any applicable course of dealing or performance or usage of trade must be construed whenever reasonable as consistent with one another, when that construction is unreasonable, express terms control. § 1-303(e). However, it can be difficult to determine whether the implied term is consistent with the express term. Thus, where leases clearly specified the rent and term, there was no room for a contrary construction (although consistent with a claimed usage of trade) that the lessee could return the leased equipment prior to the end of the lease term and terminate liability for the rent. *State ex rel. Conley Lott Nichols Mach. Co. v. Safeco Ins. Co. of America,* 671 P.2d 1151, 38 U.C.C. Rep. Serv. 423 (N.M. App. 1983). A similar conclusion was reached in *First Nat'l Bank of Atoka v. Calvin Pickle Co.,* 11 U.C.C. Rep. Serv. 1245 (Okla. App. 1973), *rev'd on other grounds,* 516 P.2d 265, 12 U.C.C. Rep. Serv. 943 (Okla. 1973) (lender had consented to the sale of crops in the past but the security agreement at issue provided the collateral could not be sold without the secured party's written consent). See also *Golden Peanut Co. v. Hunt,* 203 Ga. App. 469, 416 S.E.2d 896, 18 U.C.C. Rep. Serv. 2d 26 (1992) (while a written contract may be explained or supplemented by usage of trade evidence, such evidence may not alter or vary the express terms of the contract).

In the notorious case of *Columbia Nitrogen Corp. v. Royster Co.,* 451 F.2d 3 (4th Cir. 1971) (applying Virginia law), the contract provided for the sale of phosphate at a specified price. When the market collapsed, the buyer sought to pay a lower price, claiming that due to trade usage and course of dealing, the express terms were merely projections that could be adjusted according to market forces. The district court held that the evidence should be excluded because it would contradict the express price term of the agreement. The appellate court reversed, however, finding that the evidence was not inconsistent with the express term. There is something to be said for the decision. If the price had been stated as $10,000, then evidence that the price was $8,000 would clearly be inconsistent. But if the provision had expressly stated, "The price is $10,000. The price is a projection that can be adjusted according to market forces," then the buyer would have a good argument. So it may be an equally good argument that the additional language is supplied by trade usage and course of dealing.

Courts have nevertheless expressed dissatisfaction with the outcome of *Columbia Nitrogen.* See *Southern Concrete Services, Inc. v. Mableton Contractors, Inc.*, 407 F. Supp. 581, 19 U.C.C. Rep. Serv. 79 (N.D. Ga. 1975) (applying Georgia law) ("Certainly customs of the trade should be relevant to the interpretation of certain terms of a contract, and should be considered in determining what variation in specifications is considered acceptable, but this court does not believe that Section 2-202 was meant to invite a frontal assault on the essential terms of a clear and explicit contract.") and *Sagent Tech., Inc. v. Micros Sys.*, 276 F. Supp. 2d 464, 51 U.C.C. Rep. Serv. 2d 59 (D. Md. 2003) (applying Maryland law) ("Additional terms are inconsistent with a written document if the additional terms are not reasonably harmonious with the 'language and respective obligations of the parties.' Terms that impose new legal obligations on or alter the existing legal obligations of the parties, like those proffered by MSI, are not reasonably harmonious with the terms of a written agreement.").

G. The Code Hierarchy

Trade usage and course of dealing or performance should be construed if at all possible as consistent with each other and with the express terms of an agreement. However, if that is unreasonable, the interpretation of the contract should occur with the following priority: express terms, course of performance, course of dealing, and usage of trade. See § 1-303(e).

In this hierarchy, express terms ultimately control, and in their absence, course of performance prevails over the other two and course of dealing over usage of trade. The theory is that the one closest to the parties' manifestations governs. See, e.g., *Farmers State Bank v. Farmland Foods, Inc.*, 225 Neb. 1, 402 N.W2d 277, 3 U.C.C. Rep. Serv. 2d 902 (1987) (court stated that a course of dealing cannot override the express terms of an agreement) and *Barliant v. Follett Corp.*, 138 Ill. App. 3d 756, 483 N.E.2d 1312, 91 Ill. Dec. 677, 42 U.C.C. Rep. Serv. 1206 (1985) (even if the trade practice was that the seller paid for transportation and insurance, the course of dealing between the parties was that the seller billed the buyer for transportation and insurance and the buyer paid).

H. Express Terms Modified by Waiver

A distinction must be made between actions prior to the agreement and actions following the agreement that may amount to a waiver or modification of the express terms of the agreement. Frequently, one party will lull another by its repeated actions or inactions into thinking that the express terms will not be enforced. These actions may give rise to a waiver of the party's right to enforce the express term. See § 1-303(f). See also *J.R. Hale Contracting Co., Inc. v. United New Mexico Bank at Albuquerque*, 110 N.M. 712, 799 P.2d 581, 13 U.C.C. Rep. Serv. 2d 53 (1990) (bank accelerated a note in accordance with its terms when debtor's first payment was twenty-three days late and debtor protested that bank had not objected to late payment during the prior eleven-year commercial relationship; court held qualification of the note terms could not be implied in these circumstances from a past course of conduct).

This issue frequently arises with respect to a default under a payment plan or a default as defined in a security agreement. For example, in *Clovis Nat'l Bank v. Thomas*, 77 N.M. 554, 425 P.2d 726, 4 U.C.C. Rep. Serv. 137 (N.M. 1967), where a bank repeatedly acquiesced in the debtor's sale of cattle in spite of a provision in the security agreement that provided that "[w]ithout the prior written consent of Secured Party, Debtor will not sell, ... or otherwise dispose of the Collateral," the bank was held to have waived its right to claim that the debtor's sale of the cattle without written consent was wrongful.

I. Notice

Finally, § 1-303(g) provides that evidence of usage of trade is not admissible unless the party offering it has given the other party notice that the court finds sufficient to prevent unfair surprise.

CHAPTER

17

GOOD FAITH
§ 1-304

§ 1-304. Obligation of Good Faith.

Every contract or duty within [the Uniform Commercial Code] imposes an obligation of good faith in its performance and enforcement.

A. Introduction

Section 1-304 imposes an obligation of good faith in the performance or enforcement of every contract or duty under the Code. To be consistent with changes in other articles of the Code (except Article 5), the definition of good faith in Revised § 1-201(b)(20) has been expanded from only "honesty in fact" in former § 1-201(19) to include "the observance of reasonable commercial standards of fair dealing." Section 1-201(b)(20) provides:

> "Good faith," except as otherwise provided in Article 5, means honesty in fact and the observance of reasonable commercial standards of fair dealing.

Thus, the obligation now includes both a "subjective" element—honesty in fact—and an "objective" element—the observance of reasonable commercial standards. Since acting in good faith means satisfying *both* elements, then the obligation can be breached by failure to observe *either* element. However, a significant number of jurisdictions retain only the subjective element either because they have not enacted Revised Article 1 or they enacted it but retained the former definition. Thus, it is crucial for the practitioner to determine which definition applies in a particular jurisdiction.

A good illustration of the distinction between the two elements can be found in the case of *Neumiller Farms, Inc. v. Cornett*, 368 So. 2d 272, 26 U.C.C. Rep. Serv. 61 (Ala. 1979). Prior to the revision of Article 1, § 2-103(b) applied both the subjective and objective standards of good faith only to merchants. Because the revision applies both standards to all parties, the Article 2 provision is repealed as redundant in jurisdictions that enact Revised Article 1. The case is of particular relevance today because, since the buyer was a merchant, it applies both standards. Neumiller Farms had agreed to buy potatoes from Cornett that "chipt to buyer satisfaction"—that is, they were suitable for making potato chips. When the price of potatoes fell, Neumiller refused to purchase Cornett's potatoes, claiming breach of that warranty. An agent of Neumiller told Cornett at one point when Neumiller refused his potatoes, "I can buy potatoes all day for $2.00," thus providing evidence that it was breaching the duty as measured by the subjective standard—Neumiller was not honest because the chipping ability was not the real reason it refused to purchase the potatoes. Furthermore, Cornett had the potatoes tested by an expert from the Cooperative Extension Service, who reported that the potatoes were suitable in all respects. This expert opinion provided evidence that Neumiller also breached the duty as measured by the objective standard, for a person observing reasonable commercial standards would have accepted them.

A good illustration of how the concept generally is intended to operate is furnished by § 8-504(a). Section 8-504(a) requires a securities intermediary "to obtain and thereafter maintain a financial asset in a quantity corresponding to the aggregate of all security entitlements it has established in favor of its entitlement holders with respect to that financial asset." In short, if a broker has purchased 100,000 shares of XYZ stock for its customers, it must have that amount of XYZ stock available if those customers wish to sell or obtain share certificates. How is this statutory duty to be performed? Under § 8-504(c)(2), in the absence of agreement, it must be performed with due care in accordance with reasonable commercial standards, or under § 8-504(c)(1), as agreed upon with its customer. In this latter context, the duty of good faith limits freedom of contract. It would not be consistent with the duty of good faith for the agreement to disclaim entirely this basic element of the relationship between the broker and its customers, such as by providing that the broker assumed no responsibility for maintaining any of its customers' securities positions. § 8-504 Official Comment 4. However, the agreement, consistent with good faith and applicable government regulation, might provide that if another broker failed to make a delivery, there is a certain period of time in which to clear up the problem before the acquiring broker is obligated to obtain the necessary securities from another source. This language constitutes a determination of the standards by which good faith is to be measured, as permitted under § 1-302(b). See Chapter 15.

B. Application only to Code Contracts or Duties

The obligation of good faith applies only to a contract or duty within the Code. Thus, the Code duty (as opposed to any common law duty) does not apply to the fees charged by a bank, as the Code generally does not deal with such fees. See *Tolbert v. First Nat'l Bank of Oregon,* 312 Or. 485, 823 P.2d 965, 17 U.C.C. Rep. Serv. 2d 1204 (1991). But see § 4-406 Official Comment 3:

> Moreover, this Act does not regulate fees that banks charge their customers for furnishing items

or copies or other services covered by the Act, but under principles of law such as unconscionability or good faith and fair dealing, courts have reviewed fees and the bank's exercise of a discretion to set fees. Perdue v. Crocker National Bank, 38 Cal.3d 913 (1985) (unconscionability); Best v. United Bank of Oregon, 739 P.2d 554, 562-566 (1987) (good faith and fair dealing). In addition, Section [1-304] provides that every contract or duty within this Act imposes an obligation of good faith in its performance or enforcement.

Nor did a bank violate the duty of good faith when it employed a high to low method of posting checks, since § 4-303 allows the bank to choose any method. See *Fetter v. Wells Fargo Bank Texas, N.A.*, 110 S.W.3d 683, 51 U.C.C. Rep. Serv. 2d 201 (Tx. Ct. App. 2003). In *In re Checking Account Overdraft Litigation*, 694 F. Supp. 2d 1302, 71 U.C.C. Rep. Serv. 2d 431 (S.D. Fl. 2010), the court on a motion to dismiss held that this body of law may not be applicable to a debit card, which is not a UCC transaction. The obligation does not apply to an insurance contract (*see Elrad v. United Life & Accident Ins. Co.*, 624 F. Supp. 742, 42 U.C.C. Rep. Serv. 849 (N.D. Ill. 1985)) or to aspects of the agreement of an applicant to reimburse the issuer of a letter of credit (see § 5-102 Official Comment 3). See also PEB Commentary No. 10, February 10, 1994, note 1. On the other hand, a buyer acts in bad faith when it bars the seller from exercising the right to cure permitted by the Code and then makes a claim for breach of warranty. *Ranta Const., Inc. v. Anderson*, 190 P.3d 835, 66 U.C.C. Rep. Serv. 2d 200 (Colo. Ct. App. 2008).

The concept applies whether or not the Code section mentions good faith, but particular applications of the good faith obligation at times appear expressly in various provisions of the Code, including §§ 1-309 (acceleration "at will" must be in good faith), 2-603(3) (duties of merchant buyer with respect to rightfully rejected goods—"buyer is held only to good faith"), 2A-109 (acceleration "at will" must be in good faith), 3-418 (insulation from recovery of money erroneously paid if person took instrument in good faith), 4-209 (necessity of person asserting warranty to have taken instrument in good faith), 5-109 (good faith claimant under letter of credit not subject to nonpayment even if fraud by others involved); and 9-615(g) (junior creditor who receives cash proceeds in good faith takes the proceeds free of the security interest).

The concept also plays a role in determining whether a holder of an instrument is a holder in due course (§ 3-302(a), providing that one requirement is that the holder took the instrument in good faith), and whether the transferee of collateral after the debtor's default takes free of liens (§ 9-617(b), providing that the transferee must act in good faith to take free). But the Code duty does not extend to the *negotiation* stage; a court imposing a duty of good faith to *negotiate* must rely on other law. *Tolbert v. First Nat'l Bank of Oregon,* 312 Or. 485, 823 P.2d 965, 17 U.C.C. Rep. Serv. 2d 1204 (1991).

C. Consequences of Breaching Good Faith

What is the consequence of requiring "good faith"? Some courts have determined that there is an independent cause of action for breach of good faith with respect to the performance and enforcement of a contract. See *Quality Automotive Co. v. Signet Bank/ Maryland,* 775 F. Supp. 849, 16 U.C.C. Rep. Serv. 2d 951 (D. Md. 1991), and *Reid v. Key Bank of Southern Maine, Inc.*, 821 F.2d 9, 3 U.C.C. Rep. Serv. 2d 1665 (1st Cir. 1987) (applying ME law). This argument gets some support from § 1-305, which states in Official Comment 2: "Under subsection (b), any right or obligation described in the Uniform Commercial Code is enforceable by action, even though no remedy may be expressly provided, unless a particular provision specifies a different and limited effect."

Nevertheless, most cases and commentators reject this view. In fact, *Doyle v. Fleetwood Homes of Virginia, Inc.*, 650 F. Supp. 2d

535 (2009) (applying West Virginia law), which held that a breach of the obligation of good faith does not support an independent cause of action, cites subsequent authority in Maryland and Maine that questions the outcomes in *Quality Automotive* and *Reid*:

> *Hinman v. Brothers Volkswagen, Inc.*, No. CV–94–964, 1995 Me. Super. LEXIS 309, at *6–8 (Super. Ct. Me. Sept. 1, 1995) (holding, "Maine does not recognize an independent claim for a breach of the [U.C.C.] implied covenant of good faith."), and *Howard Oaks, Inc. v. Md. Nat'l Bank*, 810 F. Supp. 674, 677 (D. Md. 1993) (holding, "under the U.C.C. as well as the general law of Maryland, there is no independent duty of good faith in commercial dealing enforceable by an action *ex delicto*.").

The prevailing view is that the duty of good faith controls the manner in which contracting parties carry out obligations they have undertaken, but neither gives a court power to impose additional obligations on one contracting party nor creates a substantive cause of action. The section is directive rather than remedial. Official Comment 1 to § 1-304 provides in part:

> This section does not support an independent cause of action for failure to perform or enforce in good faith. Rather, this section means that a failure to perform or enforce, in good faith, a specific duty or obligation under the contract, constitutes a breach of that contract or makes unavailable, under the particular circumstances, a remedial right or power. This distinction makes it clear that the doctrine of good faith merely directs a court towards interpreting contracts within the commercial context in which they are created, performed, and enforced, and does not create a separate duty of fairness and reasonableness which can be independently breached.

Authorities supporting this view include *U and W Industrial Supply, Inc. v. Martin Marietta Alumina, Inc.*, 24 U.C.C. Rep. Serv. 2d 421 (3rd Cir. 1994) (applying Virgin Islands law) (good faith obligation controls the manner in which parties carry out their contractual obligations and does not give a court power to impose additional obligations), and *Gov't St. Lumber Co., Inc. v. Am South Bank, N.A.*, 553 So. 2d 68, 9 U.C.C. Rep. Serv. 2d 1218 (Ala. 1989) (good faith obligation does not create a substantive action in tort or contract; it is directive rather than remedial); *In re Heartland Chemicals, Inc.*, 103 B.R. 1012, 10 U.C.C. Rep. Serv. 2d 308 (Bankr. C.D. Ill. 1989) (failure to act in good faith in and of itself does not give rise to cause of action); *Super Glue Corp. v. Avis Rent A Car System, Inc.*, 132 A.D.2d 604, 517 N.Y.S.2d 764, 4 U.C.C. Rep. Serv. 2d 385 (1987) (Code does not permit recovery of money damages for bad faith conduct when no other basis for recovery is present); *Diversified Products, Inc. v. Tops Markets, Inc.*, 2001 WL 640697, 45 U.C.C. Rep. Serv. 2d 101 (W.D.N.Y. 2001) (stating that "plaintiff's claim for breach of the implied covenant of good faith and fair dealing is not properly a separate cause of action in and of itself, but is to be considered in relation to and in conjunction with plaintiff's breach of contract claims."); *Adolph Coors Co. v. Rodriguez*, 780 S.W.2d 477, 10 U.C.C. Rep. Serv. 2d 299 (Tex. App. 1989) (tort action for breach of good faith may arise when the parties have a "special relationship," but because the ordinary commercial contractual is not such a relationship, the alleged bad faith conduct must be related to the failure to perform some part of the contract, and gives rise to an action stated for breach of contract); and PEB Commentary No. 10, February 10, 1994.

D. Meaning of Good Faith

What does "good faith" mean? "Good faith" means the same thing in each article, with the exception of Article 5, in which the standard is simple honesty in fact because the narrower concept appropriately reinforces rather than erodes the "independence" principle central to letters of credit, the subject of Article 5. § 5-102 Official Comment 3.

"Honesty in fact" includes adherence to a course of performance, a course of dealing, the parties' clear intent, and the express practice of the industry. *Watseka First Nat'l Bank v. Ruda,* 135 Ill. 2d 140, 552 N.E.2d 775, 10 U.C.C. Rep. Serv. 2d 1073 (1990), and PEB Commentary No. 10, February 10, 1994. It means acting on what one believes one knows, whether or not what is believed is actual fact. *Rigby Corp. v. Boatmen's Bank & Trust Co.,* 713 S.W.2d 517, 4 U.C.C. Rep. Serv. 2d 19 (Mo. App. 1986). Acting in good faith excludes fraud (*In re Amica, Inc.,* 135 B.R. 534, 17 U.C.C. Rep. Serv. 2d 11 (Bankr. N.D. Ill. 1992)), unconscionability (*In re Jackson,* 9 U.C.C. Rep. Serv. 1152 (W.D. Mo., Ref., 1971)), and a design to mislead or deceive as well as action with a purpose to deprive another of valid rights (*Bunge Corp. v. Recker,* 519 F.2d 449, 17 U.C.C. Rep. Serv. 400 (8th Cir. 1975) (applying MO law), and *In re Everett Home Town Ltd. P'ship,* 146 B.R. 453, 19 U.C.C. Rep. Serv. 2d 874 (Bankr. Ariz. 1992)).

On the other hand, willful disregard of suspicious facts cannot be tolerated. *Kotis v. Nowlin Jewelry, Inc.,* 844 S.W.2d 920, 19 U.C.C. Rep. Serv. 2d 1067 (Tex. App. 1992), and *Community Bank v. Ell,* 278 Ore. 417, 564 P.2d 685, 21 U.C.C. Rep. Serv. 1349 (1977). Moreover, the determination of whether a person lacked a good faith belief should be based on facts and circumstances surrounding the transaction and not solely on the person's testimony concerning state of mind. Thus, even under a subjective test of good faith, when the trier of fact evaluates credibility, the fact finder may take into account the reasonableness of the assertion of good faith. *Funding Consultants, Inc. v. Aetna Casualty & Surety Co.,* 187 Conn. 637, 447 A.2d 1163 (1982) and *J.R. Hale Contracting Co., Inc. v. United New Mexico Bank at Albuquerque,* 110 N.M. 712, 799 P.2d 581, 13 U.C.C. Rep. Serv. 2d 53 (1990).

The subjective definition should not be supplemented by any broader common law definition. See *United States Nat'l Bank of Oregon v. Boge,* 311 Or. 550, 814 P.2d 1082, 15 U.C.C. Rep. Serv.

2d 24 (1991) and *Bank of America, N.A. v. Prestige Imports*, 75 Mass. App. Ct. 741, 917 N.E.2d 207, 71 U.C.C. Rep. Serv. 2d 135 (2009) (holding that the trial court judge's instruction was erroneous because it was not limited to the conscious and purposeful wrongdoing required for a finding of bad faith, but included negligence, recklessness, and commercially unreasonable conduct).

While there are cases that have ignored the narrower definition under former law, such as *In re Martin Specialty Vehicles, Inc.,* 87 B.R. 752, 6 U.C.C. Rep. Serv. 2d 337 (Bankr. D. Mass. 1988) (fairness, not just honesty, is evaluated), and *Star Credit Corp. v. Molina,* 59 Misc. 2d 290, 298 N.Y.S.2d 570, 6 U.C.C. Rep. Serv. 70 (N.Y. Civ. Ct. 1969) (good faith means more than honesty when assignee seeks to bar assertion of consumer claim), such judicial activism is no longer necessary. In the case of Article 5, which retains the narrower subjective meaning, an expansive view would not be appropriate. See § 5-102 Official Comment 3 for an explanation of why the narrower view of good faith is necessary to protect the "independence" principle.

E. Application of the Concept

To illustrate the application of the honesty in fact part of the concept, each party to a sales contract must act in good faith, and a buyer under a contract in which the seller has agreed to deliver the required goods is not acting in good faith if it insists on delivery of unneeded goods—even if at the time delivery was first requested the buyer's actual requirements were for the larger quantity. *Homestake Mining Co. v. Washington Public Power Supply System,* 476 F. Supp. 1162, 26 U.C.C. Rep. Serv. 1113 (N.D. Calif. 1979).

An automobile dealer was not acting in good faith when it accepted the buyer's check for a car, gave the buyer a bill of sale identifying the car by model and serial number, and then refused to deliver the car, claiming the car in his possession was not the same type as ordered by the buyer. *Tatum v. Richter,* 280 Md. 332, 373 A.2d 923, 21 U.C.C. Rep. Serv. 967 (1977). Other applications include *Thompson v. United States,* 408 F.2d 1075, 6 U.C.C. Rep. Serv. 20 (8th Cir. 1969) (applying Arkansas law), in which a family corporation sold furniture to a family partnership on unsecured credit. The partnership installed the furniture in an apartment project operated by the partnership. The partnership also had given a prior security interest on the project, which included all furniture, but which was not filed to perfect the security interest in the furniture as to third parties. When the partnership went into default, it executed a second security interest in the furniture to the corporation, which was properly filed. Under §§ 9-201 and 9-317(a)(l), this would give the corporation a prior right in the furniture over the first secured party. However, the court held that, under the circumstances, for the corporation to enforce its security interest over the earlier security interest would be an act of bad faith by the family members, who were the same persons in both the corporation and the partnership.

In *First Nat'l Bank. v. Twombly,* 213 Mont. 66, 689 P.2d 1226, 39 U.C.C. Rep. Serv. 1192 (Mont. 1984), the bank made a loan to a small business. When the business was sold, a bank officer agreed to permit it to be paid in installments, instead of at its one-year maturity. After the business was sold, however, the bank insisted on payment even earlier than original maturity on the ground that the asserted right to payment in installments, even though promised by a bank officer (who was out of town), together with the sale of the business rendered payment uncertain at maturity. The court found the bank had not acted in good faith.

Much litigation over good faith has centered on acceleration clauses, as in the *Twombly* case. Section 1-309 allows acceleration of payment or performance when a person acting in good faith deems itself insecure. See Chapter 22. Most cases decided under former Article 1 held that this means there is a power to do so when the person honestly believes the prospect of payment or performance is impaired, even if evidence viewed objectively indicates in fact there is no insecurity. *Karner v. Willis,* 10 Kan. App. 2d 432, 700 P.2d 582, 41 U.C.C. Rep. Serv. 721 (1985) (test of good faith is subjective requiring only honesty in fact, and good faith may be present even though evidence presented, viewed objectively, indicates that the bank is not in fact insecure); *Farmers Cooperative Elevator, Inc. v. State Bank,* 236 N.W.2d 674, 18 U.C.C. Rep. Serv. 607 (Iowa 1975) (good faith required by § 1-208 (now § 1-309) does not require, in addition to honesty in fact, a reasonable belief in impairment of the prospect of payment); and *Rigby Corp. v. Boatmen's Bank & Trust Co.,* 713 S.W.2d 517, 4 U.C.C. Rep. Serv. 2d 19 (Mo. App. 1986) (a creditor acts in good faith in accelerating a debt if he acts on what he believes he knows, whether or not what he believes is actual, as long as the belief is not bereft of rational basis and does not amount to an open abuse of the creditor's discretionary power).

Some cases have questioned whether there is any difference between the two standards. However, these cases must be reviewed in light of Revised Article 1, which requires adherence to both the subjective and objective standard. In *Reid v. Key Bank of Southern Maine, Inc.,* 821 F.2d 9, 3 U.C.C. Rep. Serv. 2d 1665 (1st Cir. 1987) (applying Maine law), a case that arose under former Article 1, the bank argued that the judge had erroneously instructed the jury on both standards, but the court suggested in a footnote that the two standards could be conflated:

> Moreover, we think there are strong indications that such a limitation [to the subjective standard] would not represent the Maine court's future, or even current, thinking on this matter. First, we note that many courts have construed the "good faith" provision of [§ 1-309] as including an objective component. *See, e.g.,* K.M.C. Co. v. Irving Trust Co., 757 F.2d 752, 760-61 (6th Cir.1985). This construction was supported by the views of Professor Gilmore, one of the drafters of the U.C.C. *See* 2 G. Gilmore, *Security Interests in Personal Property* 43.4 at 1197 (1965). *See also* J. White and R. Summers, *Uniform Commercial Code*

1088 (2d ed.1980) ("The draftsmen apparently intended an objective standard."). Moreover, as many commentators have shown, the difference between so-called "objective" and "subjective" standards is often minimal in practice. *See, e.g.,* J. White and R. Summers at 1088-90.

Courts generally agree that a party does not violate a duty of good faith by adhering to its agreement or by enforcing its legal and contractual rights. Courts are often called upon to apply the concept when one party has discretionary authority to determine certain terms of the contract, such as quantity, price, or time. Compare *Amoco Oil Co. v. Ervin,* 908 P.2d 493, 28 U.C.C. Rep. Serv. 2d 452 (Colo. 1995) (court found that "the duty of good faith cannot be used to contradict terms or conditions for which a party has bargained") with *ADT Security Services, Inc. v. Premier Home Protection, Inc.,* 181 P.3d 288, 64 U.C.C. Rep. Serv. 2d 178 (Colo. 2007) (court concluded that one party's conduct was not contrary to the justified expectations of the other as established by the language of the contract).

As an example of this concept, the duty of good faith does not apply to demand instruments, which give the creditor the right to demand payment at any time. See *Diversified Foods, Inc. v. First Nat'l Bank of Boston,* 605 A.2d 609, 17 U.C.C. Rep. Serv. 2d 1028 (Me. 1992) and Official Comment 1 to § 1-309, which states:

Obviously this section has no application to demand instruments or obligations whose very nature permits call at any time with or without reason. This section applies only to an obligation of payment or performance which in the first instance is due at a future date.

See also *Creeger Brick & Building Supply, Inc. v. Mid-State Bank & Trust Co.,* 385 Pa. Super. 30, 560 A.2d 151, 9 U.C.C. Rep. Serv. 2d 438 (1989). See also *Waller v. Maryland Nat. Bank,* 95 Md. App. 197, 620 A.2d 381, 20 U.C.C. Rep. Serv. 2d 492 (1993) (duty of good faith did not change the terms of parties' contract, the clear and unambiguous language of which provided that payment was to be on demand); *Shawmut Bank, N.A. v. Miller,* 415 Mass. 482, 614 N.E.2d 668, 21 U.C.C. Rep. Serv. 2d 13 (1993) (parties to a loan could agree that the lender could collect the balance due on a demand note at will without the application of an unbargained for obligation of good faith); and *In re Nantahala Village, Inc.,* 976 F.2d 876, 18 U.C.C. Rep. Serv. 2d 1027 (4th Cir. 1992) (where lender's conduct flowed from valid and binding loan documents, lender had not violated duty of good faith merely by exercising its contract rights).

Of course, under §§ 1-304, 1-309, and 1-201(b)(20), the acceleration provision requiring good faith now includes the observance of reasonable commercial standards of fair dealing. Nevertheless, cases applying the subjective standard should still be good law, so long as the conduct involved does not transgress reasonable commercial standards of fair dealing. The honesty in fact part of the good faith concept is likely to remain of central importance, given the probable difficulty of establishing more general content for the reasonable commercial standards part of the concept.

Fair dealing is viewed as broader than honesty in fact. One can be honest but unfair when measured against what most others do. The broader, more objective standard requires conformity with accepted norms in the context involved. For example, suppose an insurer tenders a check in settlement of a personal injury claim in an accident that appears to be covered under the policy without much doubt. Suppose further the claimant is necessitous and the amount of the check is very small in relation to the injury and the amount possibly recoverable under the policy. The trier of fact might conclude that the insurer was taking unfair advantage of the claimant, and the resulting accord and satisfaction might not be effective. See § 3-311 Official Comment 4, § 2-209 Official Comment 2, and *Dhiman v. Rockford Industries, Inc.,* 42 U.C.C. Rep. Serv. 2d 767 (N.D. Ill. 2000). As alluded to in Chapter 15 in connection with limitation on agreements, while the parties may define the standard by which the statutory duties of a securities intermediary may be performed under §§ 8-504 through 8-508, the fair dealing standard precludes them from disclaiming altogether one of the basic duties that define that relationship. See § 8-504 Official Comment 4.

However, beyond these examples, the import of the extended concept becomes less clear. For an illustration, see *Maine Family Federal Credit Union v. Sun Life Assur. Co. of Canada,* 37 U.C.C. Rep. Serv. 2d 875 (Maine 1999) (court used the new standard to question holder in due course status for a financial institution that made uncollected funds available to its customer even though in compliance with federal Regulation CC and seemingly consistent with virtually unanimous prior case law, such as *Friendly Nat'l Bank of Southwest Oklahoma City v. Farmers Ins. Group,* 630 P.2d 318 (Okla. 1981)). Moreover, while much case law, such as *Money Mart Cashing Center, Inc. v. Epicycle Corp.,* 667 P.2d 1372 (Colo. 1983) and *Georg v. Metro Fixtures Contractors, Inc.,* 178 P.3d 1209, 66 U.C.C. Rep. Serv. 2d 477 (Colo. 2008), holds that no general duty to inquire as to the instrument or the underlying obligation resides in the duty of good faith, even if some suspicious circumstances exist, § 9-331 Official Comment 5 suggests there may be circumstances in which reasonable commercial standards of fair dealing do require a form of inquiry.

Of course, if a person fails to make an inquiry for the purpose of remaining ignorant of facts that the person believes would disclose a problem in the transaction, there may be bad faith. See *General Investment Corp. v. Angelini,* 58 N.J. 396, 278 A.2d 193, 9 U.C.C. Rep. Serv. 1 (1971) and *Triffin v. Pomerantz Staffing Services LLC,* 370 N.J. Super. 301, 851 A.2d 100, 53 U.C.C. Rep. Serv. 2d 927 (2004). However, whether an established duty of affirmative inquiry can ever be contained is quite another matter. It should be noted, though, that failure to exercise ordinary care in conducting a transaction is an entirely different concept than that of good faith. See § 3-103 Official Comment 4 and *Halla v. Norwest Bank Minnesota, N.A.,* 601 N.W.2d 449 (Minn. App. 1999).

F. Question of Fact

Good faith generally is not a question of law but a question of fact. *McKay v. Farmers & Stockmens Bank of Clayton*, 92 N.M. 181, 585 P.2d 325, 24 U.C.C. Rep. Serv. 517 (N.M. App. 1978) (good faith generally is a question of fact, not law), and *Fort Knox Nat'l Bank v. Gustafson*, 385 S.W.2d 196, 2 U.C.C. Rep. Serv. 336 (Ky. 1964) (submission to the jury of the issue of good faith is required unless the evidence relating to it is insignificant or lacks probative value). Thus, because the inquiry is so fact-intensive, it can be difficult to predict from prior cases how a court will rule on a particular case.

CHAPTER

18

REMEDIES ADMINISTERED
§ 1-305

---

§ 1-305. Remedies to Be Liberally Administered.

(a) The remedies provided by [the Uniform Commercial Code] must be liberally administered to the end that the aggrieved party may be put in as good a position as if the other party had fully performed but neither consequential or special damages nor penal damages may be had except as specifically provided in [the Uniform Commercial Code] or by other rule of law.

(b) Any right or obligation declared by [the Uniform Commercial Code] is enforceable by action unless the provision declaring it specifies a different and limited effect.

A. Liberal Administration of Remedies

Section 1-305(a) states an overall policy of liberality of remedy, but with significant limitations which may come into play in a variety of circumstances. The provision first states that remedies provided by the Code are intended to be liberally administered so that the position of an injured party will be as good as if the other party had fully performed. In contract law, this goal is known as the "expectancy" or the "expectation interest."

For example, suppose a seller breaches a sales contract. The Code in §§ 2-712 and 2-713 gives the buyer a choice of remedy between cover damages and market damages so that in a rising market the buyer will not be prejudiced if the cost of the goods increases between the time of breach and the time the buyer acquires substitute goods. But suppose the buyer is a middleman and, instead of measuring damages by the lost profit on its resale contracts under § 2-712, the buyer seeks damages under § 2-713 measured by the difference between the contract and market prices, which is an amount greater than the actual loss. Former § 1-106 was used to limit the recovery on facts similar to these in *Allied Canners & Packers, Inc. v. Victor Packing Co.,* 162 Cal. App. 3d 905, 209 Cal. Rptr. 60, 39 U.C.C. Rep. Serv. 1567 (1984) and the reasoning of *Allied* was followed in *NHF Hog Marketing, Inc. v. Pork-Martin LLP*, 811 N.W.2d 116, 76 U.C.C. Rep. Serv. 2d 480 (Minn. Ct. App. 2012) under § 1-305(a). However, in *Tongish v. Thomas,* 251 Kan. 728, 840 P.2d 471, 20 U.C.C. Rep. Serv. 2d 936 (1992), in a thoughtful opinion, the court distinguished *Allied* and awarded market damages even though the actual cover loss was smaller.

This section has been employed in other contexts in *Elmhurst Auto Parts, Inc. v. Fencl-Tufo Chevrolet, Inc.,* 235 Ill. App. 3d 88, 600 N.E.2d 1229, 19 U.C.C. Rep. Serv. 2d 584 (1992) (concept of liberal administration of remedies dictated conclusion that supplemental proceeding to discover assets tolled the statute of limitations); *Clark v. Associates Commercial Corp.,* 820 F. Supp. 562, 21 U.C.C. Rep. Serv. 2d 860 (D. Kan. 1993) (debtor denied replevin even though collateral wrongfully repossessed through breach of peace, as to grant replevin when debtor in default would put debtor in better position than correct performance by secured party); *Bank of Chapmanville v. Workman,* 406 S.E.2d 58, 15 U.C.C. Rep. Serv. 2d 381 (W. Va. 1991); and *Emmons v. Burkett,* 256 Ga. 855, 353

S.E.2d 908, 3 U.C.C. Rep. Serv. 2d 897 (1987) (absolute bar rule against deficiency when secured party does not conform to Article 9 inconsistent with policy of former § 1-106; now *see* §§ 9-625 and 9-626); *Chronister Oil Co. v. Unocal Refining & Marketing,* 34 F.3d 462, 24 U.C.C. Rep. Serv. 2d 485 (7th Cir. 1994) (applying Illinois law) (when buyer actually benefitted from seller's breach, buyer only entitled to nominal damages); *Abex Corp./Jetway Division v. Controlled Systems, Inc.,* 983 F.2d 1055 (Table), 1993 WL 4836, 22 U.C.C. Rep. Serv. 2d 166 (4th Cir. 1993) (applying West Virginia law) (award of prejudgment interest necessary to place supplier in position that would have resulted from performance); and *Watts v. Mercedes-Benz USA, LLC,* 254 S.W.3d 422, 63 U.C.C. Rep. Serv. 2d 966 (Tenn. Ct. App. 2007) (refusing to allow buyer to exercise right of revocation under § 2-608 against distributor where buyer had other remedies available).

Section 1-305(a) also provides that "neither consequential or special damages nor penal damages may be had except as specifically provided in [the Uniform Commercial Code] or by other rule of law." See *Bank of New York v. Amoco Oil Co.,* 35 F.3d 643, 24 U.C.C. Rep. Serv. 2d 209 (2nd Cir. 1994) (applying NY law) (court stated in dicta that because UCC Article 7 makes no reference to consequential damages, such damages are not available under Article 7). But see *Georgia Ports Authority v. Servac Int'l,* 202 Ga. App. 777, 415 S.E.2d 516, 17 U.C.C. Rep. Serv. 2d 869 (1992). Similar determinations that particular damages were unavailable occurred in *Abex Corp./Jetway Division v. Controlled Systems, Inc.* (no recovery of consequential damages as Code does not provide for such damages for a seller) and *Sullivan Indus., Inc. v. Double Seal Glass Co., Inc.,* 192 Mich. App. 333, 480 N.W.2d 623, 17 U.C.C. Rep. Serv. 2d 61 (1991) (UCC does not specifically authorize recovery of exemplary damages in breach of warranty actions, and other Michigan law bars them in breach of contract actions). However, see *Seaton v. Lawson Chevrolet-Mazda, Inc.,* 821 S.W.2d 137, 16 U.C.C. Rep. Serv. 2d 1070 (Tenn. 1991) (court held that when rescission of sales contract was based on fraud, the Code does not preclude the award of punitive damages), and *Flavor-Inn, Inc. v. NCNB Nat'l Bank of South Carolina*, 424 S.E.2d 534, 19 U.C.C. Rep. Serv. 2d 1116 (S.C. App. 1992) and *Contour Industries, Inc. v. U.S. Bancorp*, 2008 WL 2704431, 66 U.C.C. Rep. Serv. 2d 175 (E.D. Tenn. 2008) (court found punitive damages recoverable in claim under § 3-419 [revised § 3-420], which incorporates the law of conversion). White & Summers in § 8-16 argue that a seller should be allowed to recover consequential damages and make a somewhat strained argument that this would be consistent with the Code since the common law permits the recovery, and the common law is "other rule of law" encompassed by the language of § 1-305(a).

B. Enforcement by Action

At first blush, § 1-305(b) seems to state the obvious—the old maxim that for every right there is a remedy—and that view is merely reiterated by the first sentence of Official Comment 2, which states:

> Under subsection (b), any right or obligation described in the Uniform Commercial Code is enforceable by action, even though no remedy may be expressly provided, unless a particular provision specifies a different and limited effect.

One issue that has arisen under this subsection is whether the obligation of good faith found in § 1-304 is in itself "enforceable by action." While some cases have found that breach of the obligation of good faith gives rise to an independent action, the prevailing view is that it does not. See PEB Commentary No. 10, February 10, 1994, and the discussion of good faith in Chapter 17. In fact, Official Comment 1 to § 1-304 states that the doctrine "does not create a separate duty of fairness and reasonableness which can be independently breached."

Another issue raised by this subsection is the extent to which equitable relief is available as a remedy. Because the definition of "action" in § 1-201(b)(2) states that action "includes ... suit in equity," it could be argued that this provision is stating that any right or obligation in the Code is enforceable by a suit in equity. See, e.g., *Burtman v. Technical Chemicals and Products, Inc.*, 724 So. 2d 672, 37 U.C.C. Rep. Serv. 2d 753 (Fla. Dist. Ct. App. 1999) (statutory obligation to register a security transfer is enforceable by injunction). Such a view is contradicted by the second sentence of Official Comment 2, which states:

> Whether specific performance or other equitable relief is available is determined not by this section but by specific provisions and by supplementary principles. Cf. Sections 1-103, 2-716.

Of course, as discussed in Chapter 2, the language of the statute prevails over the language of the comments, so this limitation may not be meaningful. On the other hand, the definitions in § 1-201(b) must be read in the light of the limiting language in § 1-201(a), which states that the defined words have that meaning "[u]nless the context otherwise requires." The Official Comment could be read as clarifying that in this context, "action" does not necessarily include suits in equity, which have historically been constrained.

CHAPTER

19

WAIVER OR RENUNCIATION
§ 1-306

---

§ 1-306. Waiver or Renunciation of Claim or Right After Breach.

A claim or right arising out of an alleged breach may be discharged in whole or in part without consideration by agreement of the aggrieved party in an authenticated record.

Section 1-306 makes consideration unnecessary for the effective renunciation or waiver of rights or claims arising out of an alleged breach of contract if the renunciation or waiver is in a record authenticated by the party asserting the breach. The change from the requirement of a *signed writing* in former § 1-107 to an *authenticated record* in Revised § 1-306 brings Article 1 into line with the same change already accomplished by either the state Uniform Electronic Transactions Act (UETA) or the federal Electronic Signatures in Global and National Commerce Act (E-Sign). See Chapter 10. Of course, an oral renunciation or waiver may be valid if sustained by consideration, but not otherwise. *Upper*

Avenue Nat'l Bank v. First Arlington Nat'l Bank, 81 Ill. App. 3d 208, 400 N.E.2d 1105, 28 U.C.C. Rep. Serv. 615 (1980).

The provision does not apply to a modification *prior* to breach. See §§ 2-209 and 2A-208. Official Comment 3 to § 2-209 provides in part:

> "Modification or rescission" includes abandonment or other change by mutual consent…; it does not include unilateral "termination" or "cancellation" as defined in Section 2-106.

Because the party is not an "aggrieved party," the provision does not apply when the waiving party has no right or claim to waive but has only an obligation to perform. *Farmers & Stockmens Bank of Clayton v. Stafford,* 738 P.2d 60, 3 U.C.C. Rep. Serv. 2d 1311 (Colo. App. 1987).

In all cases, whether there is a renunciation or waiver is a matter of interpretation. In *National Cash Register Co. v. UNARCO Indus., Inc.,* 490 F.2d 285, 13 U.C.C. Rep. Serv. 1027 (7th Cir. 1974) (applying Illinois law), plaintiff sent defendant supplier of goods a letter stating, "we are cancelling without charge and making arrangements to procure elsewhere." When plaintiff sued for damages, defendant claimed this letter constituted a waiver or renunciation. The court held that on a motion to dismiss, this determination could not be made as a matter of law, particularly in light of § 2-720, which provides that:

> Unless the contrary intention clearly appears, expressions of "cancellation" or "rescission" of the contract or the like shall not be construed as a renunciation or discharge of any claim in damages for an antecedent breach.

See also *SEB S.A. v. Sunbeam Corp.,* 148 Fed. Appx. 774, 2005 WL 1926418 (11th Cir. 2005) (applying Florida law).

CHAPTER

20

EVIDENCE BY THIRD-PARTY
DOCUMENTS § 1-307

---

§ 1-307. Prima Facie Evidence by Third-Party Documents.

A document in due form purporting to be a bill of lading, policy or certificate of insurance, official weigher's or inspector's certificate, consular invoice, or any other document authorized or required by the contract to be issued by a third party is prima facie evidence of its own authenticity and genuineness and of the facts stated in the document by the third party.

Section 1-307 is procedural and provides that a document authorized or required by the contract to be issued by a third party, if in due form, is prima facie evidence of its authenticity and genuineness, and of the facts stated in the document. Therefore, the Code establishes that the document is admissible and the evidentiary weight to be given to it. However, merely because the document is prima facie evidence does not compel a finding of genuineness or accordance with the facts stated, nor does it preclude a contrary finding. It is up to non-Code law to determine how the prima facie case may be rebutted, and who has the burden of proceeding and the burden of proof. Official Comment 3 states:

> The provisions of this section go no further than establishing the documents in question as prima facie evidence and leave to the court the ultimate determination of the facts where the accuracy or authenticity of the documents is questioned. In this connection the section calls for a commercially reasonable interpretation.

See *Societe Generale v. Federal Ins. Co. v. Flota Mercante Grancolombiana, S.A.,* 856 F.2d 461, 6 U.C.C. Rep. Serv. 2d 1236 (2nd Cir. 1988) (applying New York law) (party could not be estopped by this provision from denying validity of bills of lading that all parties conceded were false); *Plastileather Corp. v. Aetna Casualty & Surety Co.,* 361 Mass. 356, 280 N.E.2d 402, 10 U.C.C. Rep. Serv. 956 (1972) (a clean bill of lading stating goods were in apparent good order and condition did not compel a finding that bale contents had not been damaged by water); and *Industria De Calcados Martini Ltda. v. Maxwell Shoe Co., Inc.,* 36 Mass. App. 268, 630 N.E.2d 299, 23 U.C.C. Rep. Serv. 2d 89 (1994) (third-party certificate of inspection stating shoes complied with contract did not establish the conformity of the goods against contrary evidence).

The provision applies only in contract actions governed by the Code and to "document[s] authorized or required by the contract to be issued by a third party"; it does not apply to documents prepared by the parties to the contract nor to documents prepared by third parties that, although relevant to the contract, were not authorized or required by the contract. *Thrifty Rent-A-Car Sys. v. Chuck Ruwart Chevrolet, Inc.,* 500 P.2d 172, 11 U.C.C. Rep. Serv. 734 (Colo. App. 1972), and *Paripovich v. Hayden-Murphy Equip. Co.,* 358 N.W.2d 67, 40 U.C.C. Rep. Serv. 22 (Minn. App. 1984).

CHAPTER

21

PERFORMANCE OR ACCEPTANCE UNDER RESERVATION OF RIGHTS
§ 1-308

---

§ 1-308. Performance or Acceptance Under Reservation of Rights.

(a) A party that with explicit reservation of rights performs or promises performance or assents to performance in a manner demanded or offered by the other party does not thereby prejudice the rights reserved. Such words as "without prejudice," "under protest," or the like are sufficient.

(b) Subsection (a) does not apply to an accord and satisfaction.

Section 1-308 allows a party to perform, promise performance, or accept performance of a contract in dispute in a manner demanded or offered by the other party, without waiving any rights, by the use of appropriate language reserving rights. For example, in the notorious "chicken" case, *Frigaliment Importing Co. v. B.N.S. Int'l Sales Corp.*, 190 F. Supp. 116 (S.D.N.Y. 1960), the seller claimed that it was justified in shipping a second installment of stewing chicken because the buyer had never objected to the first installment; the buyer, however, claimed that it had sent a cable to the seller explaining that it was accepting the chicken under protest and did not reject it because it needed chicken to supply to third parties. To prevent a waiver of rights, the reservation of rights must be "explicit." The provision does not require any particular language, stating:

> Words such as "without prejudice," "under protest," or the like are sufficient.

Nevertheless, it would be best to use these safe harbor terms to avoid any dispute about whether the language used was "explicit." Although not required by the provision, it would be best to memorialize the language in a record.

Section 1-308 is applicable only to Code transactions, such as sales of goods. It therefore does not apply to a disputed claim under a service contract. See § 1-102, discussed in Chapter 3.

This simple device can be useful in those cases in which a seller's withholding performance or a buyer's rejecting performance could substantially increase the damage done or suffered. On the other hand, only a waivable right or claim can be lost. The provision is probably based on what a reasonable person has been led to believe, and the fact that a buyer accepts a nonconforming tender without taking advantage of this provision does not necessarily mean that rights are waived as long as the buyer informs the other party of the breach in a reasonable time. See, e.g., *Mid-South Packers, Inc. v. Shoney's, Inc.*, 761 F.2d 1117, 41 U.C.C. Rep. Serv. 38 (5th Cir. 1985) (applying Michigan law), where a court held that a buyer which placed orders at the seller's new increased price could not later deduct the difference between the old and new prices from the amount owed the seller. The court stated:

> Shoney's ordered at and paid the new price with the intention of causing Mid-South to believe that Shoney's had accepted the new price so that

the shipments would continue; and Mid-South attached precisely that significance to Shoney's conduct. Shoney's secretly harbored intent to later deduct the difference between the old and new price could not bind Mid-South. . . . Shoney's remedy under the circumstances was either to reserve whatever right it might have had to the old price by sending its purchase orders with an "explicit reservation," [under what is now § 1-308(a)] or find a supplier who would sell at an acceptable price.

At one time this device was used to prevent an accord and satisfaction between the parties. If the offeror tendered a check for a lesser amount in full satisfaction of an obligation, the offeree would indorse it with language such as "without prejudice," thereby indicating its intent to accept the part payment without prejudice to its claim for the full amount. The cases were divided as to whether this language was effective to prevent an accord and satisfaction when the offeree also cashed the check. However, § 1-308(b) now expressly states:

Subsection (a) does not apply to an accord and satisfaction.

An accord and satisfaction is now governed by the common law and by § 3-311 when the accord and satisfaction is by check. Therefore, a party who is offered a lesser performance to settle a good faith dispute must either reject the partial performance and keep its full claim, or accept the tendered lesser performance in full satisfaction of the obligation. Thus, many cases decided with reference to this particular context are superseded.

CHAPTER

22

OPTION TO ACCELERATE AT WILL
§ 1-309

---

§ 1-309. Option to Accelerate at Will.

A term providing that one party or that party's successor in interest may accelerate payment or performance or require collateral or additional collateral "at will" or when the party "deems itself insecure," or words of similar import, means that the party has power to do so only if that party in good faith believes that the prospect of payment or performance is impaired. The burden of establishing lack of good faith is on the party against which the power has been exercised.

Many contracts contain a right to accelerate payment or performance due in installments, or to require collateral or additional collateral "at will" or under a general insecurity clause, informally known as the "Nervous Banker's Clause." Section 1-309 provides that such a right is exercisable only if the party having the right believes in good faith that the prospect of payment or performance is impaired. But see § 2A-109(2), which affords additional protection in a consumer lease. Thus, the burden of establishing lack of good faith is on the party against whom the power has been exercised, except in a consumer lease under § 2A-109(2).

The standard of good faith to be applied under Revised Article 1 is the broader standard of good faith in § 1-201(b)(20), which includes both the subjective standard of honesty and the objective standard of observance of reasonable commercial standards of fair dealing. Cases applying the standard under former Article 1, which defined good faith as including only the subjective standard, are discussed in Chapter 17, which also discusses the broader standard. In addition, see, e.g., *Smith v. Union State Bank,* 452 N.E.2d 1059, 37 U.C.C. Rep. Serv. 160 (Ct. App. Indiana 1983) (imposed objective test of reasonableness on determination of insecurity in relation to promissory note even under prior Article 3 where a subjective test should have been applied); *Bartlett Bank & Trust Co. v. McJunkins,* 147 Ill. App. 3d 52, 497 N.E.2d 398, 3 U.C.C. Rep. Serv. 2d 453 (1986) (applying subjective test but at a time when the standard for good faith was the same in both Articles 1 and 3); and *Blaine v. GMAC,* 82 Misc. 2d 653, 370 N.Y.S.2d 323, 17 U.C.C. Rep. Serv. 641 (N.Y. Co. Ct. 1975) (subjective test used in acceleration of retail installment sales contract by merchant notwithstanding § 2-103(l)(b), but the question of the wrong standard does not seem to have been raised). See also *Anderson v. Mobile Discount Corp.,* 595 P.2d 203, 26 U.C.C. Rep. Serv. 248 (Ariz. App. 1979), and *Watseka First Nat'l Bank v. Ruda,* 135 Ill. 2d 140, 552 N.E.2d 775, 10 U.C.C. Rep. Serv. 2d 1073 (1990) (court adopted the subjective standard of "did creditor have an honest belief that he was insecure, irrespective of whether that belief was reasonable").

A "general insecurity" clause gives a party the right to take an action if the party "deems itself insecure." This is a very comforting right to have and can cover uncontemplated events beyond, for example, the more specific default clauses in a secured loan agreement. The creditor's counsel should include such a clause in security agreements and promissory notes or other evidences of debt whenever possible, but should advise clients to exercise them with considerable care and an appreciation for the potential litigation that might result, particularly given the now-applicable broader standard of good faith.

CHAPTER

23

SUBORDINATED OBLIGATIONS
§ 1-310

---

§ 1-310. Subordinated Obligations.

An obligation may be issued as subordinated to performance of another obligation of the person obligated, or a creditor may subordinate its right to performance of an obligation by agreement with either the person obligated or another creditor of the person obligated. Subordination does not create a security interest as against either the common debtor or a subordinated creditor.

Subordination agreements arise frequently in commercial transactions. Debt may be subordinated on issue, or after it arises, one creditor may contractually agree that its interest is subordinated to the interest of another. For example, secured creditor A may agree to subordinate its interest to the interest of secured creditor B. See § 9-339.

The practical effect of a subordination agreement is to bring about payment to the creditor thereby given priority. For example, as described in Official Comment 2, "in the bankruptcy of the common debtor, dividends otherwise payable to the subordinated creditor are turned over to the superior creditor." Historically, different theories were presented as to why this is so. See, e.g., *Grise v. White,* 247 N.E.2d 385, 6 U.C.C. Rep. Serv. 391 (Mass. 1969). One theory was that the subordination created a security interest granted by the subordinated creditor to the superior creditor. That is, the subordination was a transaction within the meaning of what is now § 9-109 "that creates a security interest in personal property." As explained in *New York Stock Exchange v. Pickard & Co., Inc.,* 296 A.2d 143 (Del. Ch. 1972), "[t]he better theory … is that a subordination agreement is simply a contract in which a creditor (the "subordinated" or "junior" creditor) agrees that the claims of specified senior creditors must be paid in full before any payment to the subordinated debt may be made to, and retained by, the subordinated creditor."

Because of concerns that a subordination agreement might trigger application of Article 9, it was thought that the Code should settle the matter. Section 1-310 does settle it, and answers the question in the negative—"subordination does not create a security interest as against either the common debtor or a subordinated creditor." On the other hand, a subordination agreement can function as a security agreement when the intent is clearly expressed in the subordination agreement.

The "Reason for Change" in the Official Comments to former § 1-209 clarifies this history:

> The drafting history of Article 9 makes it clear that there was no intention to cover agreements by which the rights of one unsecured creditor are subordinated to the rights of another unsecured creditor of a common debtor. Nevertheless, since in insolvency proceedings dividends otherwise payable to a subordinated creditor are turned over to the superior creditor, fears have been expressed that a subordination agreement might be treated as a "security agreement" creating a "security

interest" in property of the subordinated creditor, and that inappropriate provisions of Article 9 might be applied. This optional section is intended to allay such fears by making an explicit declaration that a subordination agreement does not of itself create a security interest. Nothing in this section prevents the creation of a security interest in such a case when the parties to the agreement so intend.

CHAPTER
24

CONCLUSION

Because Article 1 applies to all transactions subject to any of the other articles of the Code (see § 1-102), the principles of Article 1 must be considered when negotiating, drafting, performing, or enforcing any transaction subject to the Code. Counsel may wish to consider the following matters in that regard:

- varying, to the extent allowed by law, the provisions of the Code by agreement, which means (a) reviewing all of the Code provisions potentially applicable to the transaction to determine if the interests of the client would be better served by a contractually established rule rather than the rule set forth in the Code, and (b) determining to what degree the Code rule may be altered. See § 1-302.
- establishing standards for the performance of the obligations of good faith, diligence, reasonableness, and care, for the time in which action must be taken, and for other obligations imposed by the Code. See §§ 1-302, 1-304, and 1-205.

- selecting, to the extent allowed by law, the jurisdiction whose laws will govern the transaction. See § 1-301.

- accepting Code definitions or, as permitted, establishing other definitions for terms, which will be particularly important if terms are used in the agreement in a manner that varies from the meaning they are given in the Code. See §§ 1-302 and 1-201.

- reviewing with the client any course of performance, course of dealing, or usage of trade that may be applicable to the transaction to determine whether it should be overridden by express terms. See § 1-303.

- reviewing other legal principles that may apply to the transaction to determine whether the parties' agreement should adopt or reject that rule or adopt a different rule. See §§ 1-302, 1-103(b), and 1-305.

- specifying the ways in which notices may be given under the agreement. See § 1-202.

- to the extent the transaction will be electronic, to the extent agreement can control, and consistent with the UETA (if enacted) and the federal E-sign law, providing appropriate provisions to replace or supplement paper-oriented rules of the Code. See § 1-108.

- including a general insecurity or similar clause giving the client the right to accelerate performance or declare a default if the client believes that the prospect of the other party's payment or performance is impaired and, to the extent possible, defining a standard for the good faith limitation upon the power, such as an honest belief after a reasonable investigation of the circumstances then present and known or reasonably discoverable. See §§ 1-302(b), 1-309.

- using the power to reserve rights in conjunction with performance or acceptance after a dispute has developed. See § 1-308.

- agreeing to discharge a claim or right after breach. See § 1-306.

APPENDIX

THE UNIFORM LAW PROCESS

by Fred H. Miller

The continuing importance of the Code suggests that a discussion of the function performed and the process employed by the ULC and the ALI, the two co-sponsors of the Code, may be useful.

The American Law Institute (ALI) has existed since 1923 and basically is composed of elected members who are attorneys and have attained distinction in the legal profession. ALI members, under the guidance of a reporter, restate the common or case law of a legal subject to clarify and otherwise facilitate the use of that law. The ALI screens proposals for projects and restatement drafts through its Council and, once a project is decided upon, appoints one or more reporters who are experts in the subject. The reporters create drafts with input from an advisory board and a members' consultative group. Drafts are considered at ALI annual meetings until the project is completed.

The Uniform Law Commission (ULC; formerly known as the National Conference of Commissioners on Uniform State Law (NCCUSL)) is an organization formed in 1892 composed of representatives (Commissioners) from each state, the District of Columbia, Puerto Rico, and the U.S. Virgin Islands. The Commissioners generally are appointed by their state governors, although some are appointed by the legislature or another state body. Commissioners serve without compensation and thus possess a degree of independent dedication to the law reform process. All Commissioners are lawyers and, by reason of the appointment process, generally are well-known members of the bar and are experienced politically, whether they are practitioners, judges, law professors, legislators, or otherwise engaged in legal pursuits. The Commissioners do their work through drafting committees that meet periodically during the year, including at an annual multiple-day meeting.

The purpose of each appointment is, with the other Commissioners from the state and other states, to determine what areas of private state law might benefit from uniformity among the states, prepare statutes to carry that object forward, and work toward the enactment of those statutes by the legislature in each jurisdiction.

The first step in the process of preparing a proposed uniform law, including the Code, is employing a study committee to examine a suggestion. Surveying each member's experience with the subject, the study committee determines whether the suggestion appears feasible and necessary and, if so, what the scope and general terms of the proposed law should be. In the case of the UCC, the suggestion and study steps often are performed by the Permanent Editorial Board and, in some cases, the American Bar Association.

If the study group recommends a revision or amendment to the Code, it must be approved by the Scope and Program and Executive Committees of ULC and the Council of the ALI before drafting begins. These "executive committees" balance the necessity and desirability of the project against available resources and schedules.

ULC has established several criteria to aid in these determinations:

- The proposed revision must appear to represent a practical step toward needed uniformity, or at least toward minimizing the diversity of state law.
- The subject matter should not be significantly novel. That is, it should not be a subject with regard to which neither legislative nor administrative experience is available.
- The subject matter should not be extremely controversial or involve important disparities in social, economic, or political policies or philosophies among the various jurisdictions. The goal is to prepare a statute for enactment—not to engage in the preparation of a model law or draft to serve as a guide or discussion piece.
- The subject normally should not involve a matter of purely local or state concern without substantial interstate implications.

Thus, proposed revisions must represent legislation that has a reasonable probability of acceptance and enactment in a substantial number of jurisdictions. In addition, given the finite resources of ULC and the ALI, preparation of proposed statutes must not require resources and preparation time beyond their probable value.

Once a decision is reached to prepare a proposed revision, a drafting committee of six to ten Commissioners and, after consultation, one or more ALI members is appointed. Some may be experts in the subject matter, but at least one will be a generalist. Lack of expertise in a subject enables generalists to raise useful questions that may not occur to the experts.

Each drafting committee has a reporter who is a legal expert in the subject of the proposed statute. The reporter collects and presents information about the subject of the proposed statute for the education and use of the drafting committee. The drafting committee determines the particular policy and provisions of the proposed statute based on (1) the information and work of the reporter, (2) advice received from various constituencies concerning those policies and provisions, and (3) experience in their practice and in the various states to the extent there is prior state legislation on the subject. The reporter then presents the policy choices in draft language. Unlike in the ALI process, the reporter does not decide what goes in the statute after receiving advice from others, but rather is the means to embody the decisions of the members of the drafting committee in appropriate statutory form.

Each drafting committee, pursuant to arrangement with the American Bar Association (ABA), also has an appointed ABA adviser. The ABA adviser collects input from every interested constituency in the ABA with respect to the proposed statute and conveys this advice to the drafting committee. The research base, knowledge, and experience of the drafting committee and its reporter thus are multiplied many times over.

In addition, other constituencies—organizations, government agencies, and trade groups—that may have an interest in the subject matter of the proposed statute are asked to send an observer to drafting committee meetings or to comment in writing on successive drafts of the statute. In this way, not only are the provisions of the proposed statute evaluated for workability against actual operations and the interests of various constituencies, but also the interchange of views during the drafting process enables each constituency to be aware of the concerns of others, elicits appreciation for those different perspectives, and assists in formulating an overall consensus about the resultant statute.

This latter point needs to be emphasized. The Code is not crafted to reflect what experts, or even the drafting committee, consider the one "right rule" or the "best position". Rather it is drafted, consistent with a range of sound policy, in consultation with the persons who will be subject to it to facilitate what they do by removing impediments that produce unnecessary expense, delay, or complexity. Thus the proposed statute does not embody an invariable truth but consists of a series of balances and compromises resulting from a democratic process.

The research and drafting efforts for a proposed revision or amendment to the Code normally require the drafting committee and its advisors and observers to meet three or four times a year for at least two years. In addition, there will be meetings with members of the ALI's consultative group to hear and consider their suggestions. The work of the drafting committee and its reporter is scrutinized and judged for balance, sensibility, and style by the entire membership of ULC at the annual meetings during each of those years and of the ALI at one or more annual meetings. Each revision must be approved by a vote of the individual jurisdictions in ULC before it is promulgated as a uniform law; the ALI membership and Council also must grant approval.

Once an amendment or revision to the Code is approved by ULC and the ALI, the Commissioners from the various states are charged with the duty of convincing the legislature in each jurisdiction to enact the uniform statute. Legislative approval seldom is an automatic process. In many states, a law revision commission or a law institute is required by law to determine the suitability of the proposed statute. This serves as a further check on the work of the Commissioners and ALI members from that state. Even in jurisdictions where such a formalized process is not required, it often occurs because somebody must determine how the proposed statute will change the present law of the jurisdiction and what conforming changes in the other law of that jurisdiction must be made. Quite commonly, this work will be accomplished by a bar association, which also will follow up enactment of the statute with appropriate continuing legal education efforts. This state-by-state process involves some risk of nonuniformity, but most states recognize that changing provisions because of local disagreement with language or nonfundamental policy is counterproductive to uniformity and can cause the national consensus to unravel. Thus, for the most part, recent proposals have been rapidly and uniformly enacted with adjustments made only to address local concerns or fundamental differences in policy particular to that state, or to adopt designated options in the uniform statute.

One may conclude from the description of the process for formulating the UCC that ULC and the ALI operate in some ways like legislatures. But characterizing the process as one of statutory rulemaking by private legislatures significantly misses the mark. A more accurate perception is that the proposed statute developed by ULC and the ALI is akin to a draft bill and that the process of developing that bill is akin to that of a legislative interim study committee presenting its conclusions in draft statutory form for consideration by the legislative body that appointed the committee.

This more appropriate perspective further provides a response to two main criticisms of the process. One is that not all interests are always represented. That is true, even though the process is open to all who wish to participate. While widespread participation clearly produces a better draft statute and a more solid and wide-based consensus for it, this participation is not absolutely necessary to a fair and balanced law. Promulgation by ULC and the ALI involves consideration of fairness and balance before the draft statute moves to the enactment process in the state legislatures.

The other criticism is that a statute reflecting the "best" rule is not always the end result. That also may be true but perhaps is inevitable in a democratic process. An adaptation of a famous observation is applicable: the process is full of deficiencies, but as over 60 years of experience with the Code appears to demonstrate, it is the best process that yet has been devised.

Fred H. Miller, the original author of this book, served for many years as Executive Director of the National Conference of Commissioners on Uniform State Laws and before that was a Commissioner from Oklahoma. He has also been chair of the Executive Committee of the Conference and president of the ULC as a Commissioner from Oklahoma. The opinions expressed in this Appendix are his and not necessarily those of the ULC, any Commissioner, or those of the present author.

ABOUT THE AUTHOR

Scott J. Burnham is the Frederick N. & Barbara T. Curley Professor of Commercial Law at Gonzaga University School of Law in Spokane, Washington. He is the author of numerous articles in the area of commercial law, and is past chair of the General Provisions Subcommittee of the Uniform Commercial Code Committee of the American Bar Association Business Law Section. He is a member of the American Law Institute.